CENTURY

First published in the UK by Century, The Random House Group Ltd,
20 Vauxhall Bridge Road, London, SW1V 2SA

Random House Australia (Pty) Limited
20 Alfred Street, Milsons Point, Sydney, New South Wales 2061, Australia

Random House New Zealand (Pty) Limited
Endulini, 5a Jubilee Road, Parktown 2193, South Africa

Random House South Africa (Pty) Limited
18 Poland Road, Glenfield, Auckland 10, New Zealand

The Random House Group Limited Reg. No. 954009

www.randomhouse.co.uk

British Library Cataloguing-in-Publication Data
A catalogue record for this book is available from the British Library

Developed and produced by Miles Kelly Publishing Ltd
Publishing Director Anne Marshall
Senior Editor Jenni Rainford
Editor Teresa Putnam
Designer James Marks
Additional Design Jo Brewer, Warris Kidwai
Text Sheri Bell-Rehwoldt, Luke Seaber, Geoff Tibballs, Tracey Turner
Copy Editor Catriona O'Shaughnessy
Indexer Helen Snaith
Picture Researcher Teresa Putnam
Image Manager Liberty Newton
Production Manager Estela Boulton
Cover Design Stuart Catterson
Colour Separation DPI Colour Digital Ltd, Saffron Walden, Essex, U.K.

ISBN 1-8441-3406-7
1 3 5 7 9 10 8 6 4 2

Printed in China

WARNING
Some of the stunts and activities in this book are undertaken by experts and should not be
attempted by anyone without adequate training and supervision.

ConTenTs

Ripley's

In December 1918, while working as a sports columnist for the *New York Globe*, Robert Ripley created his first collection of odd facts and feats. The cartoons, based on unusual athletic achievements, were submitted under the heading "Champs and Chumps," but his editor wanted a title that would describe the incredible nature of the content, so after much deliberation it was changed to "Believe It or Not!" The cartoon was an instant success and the phrase "believe it or not" soon entered everyday speech.

Robert Ripley's first "Believe It or Not!" cartoon, published in 1918.

Ripley's passion was travel and by 1940 he had visited no fewer than 201 countries. Wherever he went, he searched out the bizarre for inclusion in his syndicated newspaper cartoons, which had blossomed to reach worldwide distribution, being translated into 17 different languages and boasting a readership of 80 million people. During one trip he crossed two continents and covered over 24,000 mi (39,000 km) from New York to Cairo and back to satisfy his appetite for the weird.

Ripley was a pioneer of on-location radio broadcasting. Shown here he reports on the descent of a military parachutist using a portable telephone in Birmingham, Alabama in 1940.

" **At Chicago, one hundred people fainted every day and we had to have six beds. Here we have only three beds and hardly anyone has fainted** "

Robert Ripley comparing his 1940 New York City Odditorium to his original 1933 Chicago Odditorium

Anyone with a strange fact should contact the Ripley's web page at
www.ripleys.com

Ripley's museums

Niagara Falls, Canada

Blackpool, England

Branson, Missouri

Orlando, Florida

From the first Odditorium, built in Chicago in 1933 (where exhibits ranged from genuine shrunken heads from the Upper Amazon to *The Last Supper* painted on a dime), Ripley's remarkable collection is now showcased in 27 museums spread across nine countries.

The Ripley's TV show is syndicated around the world

Ripley's legacy lives on

Although he died in 1949 (after collapsing on the set of his weekly television show), his "Believe It or Not!" cartoons are still produced on a daily basis—just as they have been every day since 1918—making it the longest running syndicated cartoon in the world. Intrepid researchers follow in Robert Ripley's footsteps, continually scouring the world and enabling Ripley's to remain the undisputed king of the strange and unbelievable. With a huge computer database of incredible facts, people, and events, a massive photographic archive, and a warehouse stuffed with unique exhibits, Ripley's is able to present a celebration of the amazing diversity of our world, without ever passing judgment. From the outset, Robert Ripley encouraged his dedicated readers to submit material and photographs—a tradition that exists to this day. His weekly mailbag sometimes exceeded 170,000 letters! The one man who started it all was once commemorated by a memorial in his hometown church of Santa Rosa, California. The entire church was made from a single giant redwood tree...

Ripley's
VLAD
EXHIBIT NO: 22636
THE ORIGINAL DRACULA, CURRENTLY HELD AT THE NEW ORLEANS MUSEUM

Ripley's
CANNIBAL SKULL
EXHIBIT NO: 8855
DISCOVERED IN NEW GUINEA AND CURRENTLY HELD IN MYRTLE BEACH

Believe It or Not!

email hq@ripleys.com for information regarding submission, or write to Ripley Entertainment Inc., 7576 Kingspointe Parkway, #188, Orlando, Florida, 32819, U.S.A.

PiGs Might FLY

When the Olympics went to Atlanta in 1996, the media said the Games were going to be run by a bunch of rednecks.

Some locals took mild offense at this and, led by D.J. Mac Davis, staged their own annual Redneck Games in East Dublin, Georgia, to reinforce the stereotype.

Biting to Win

Apparently there is a knack to bobbing for pigs' trotters. One contestant explained, "You have to dive head-first into the water, push the trotter to the bottom of the bowl, using your face, and then bite as hard as you can on the pigs' trotter, whilst pulling your head back out."

A contestant comes up with a tasty trotter. Thank goodness no one thought of bobbing for pigs' feet at Halloween—apples are a whole lot sweeter!

A hardy Redneck Games contestant holds her breath with her head under water, in a bid to bag a winning trotter.

Another contestant strikes a perfect pose for the mud pit belly flop, while other competitors and spectators look on in awe as he dives into the pit of mud.

Eyes on the Prize

The lucky winners of the various hotly contested events at the annual Redneck Games are treated to a unique, one-of-a-kind trophy—none other than an empty, part-crushed, and mounted can of beer! Priceless—or should that be prizeless?

Events included typical redneck pastimes such as the mud pit belly flop, the hubcap hurl, a cigarette flip, a big hair contest and, the daddy of them all, the armpit serenade. Davis explains: "That's when you cup your hand under your armpit and make farting noises or tunes. In 1998, one contestant pumped out the entire theme tune to *Green Acres*!"

Here's mud in your eye... and nose and mouth and ears! He comes up muddy but unbowed and with high hopes of winning the coveted crushed beer can awarded for the best mud pit belly flop.

RED ALERT

The Redneck Games are comprised of the following events:

- Bobbing for pigs' feet
- Seed spitting
- Dumpster diving
- Hubcap hurling
- Bug zapping by spitball
- Armpit serenade
- Big-hair contest
- Mud pit belly flop
- Toilet seat throwing

On a Roller
Pariser's model is today exhibited at the Ripley Museum in South Carolina.

The Wheel Thing
Fourteen-year-old Barry Pariser, of New York, built a bridge and a ferris wheel out of 58,000 toothpicks. He worked solidly for 10 months.

Fat is a Feminist Issue
In 2004, Argentinian artist Nicola Constantino announced that she was selling sculptures made from her own body fat. More than 4 lb (2 kg) of the fat, which had been removed during liposuction, were moulded into a pair of sculptures of the female body selling at $250 (£480) apiece. She also exhibited a range of soaps made from her fat.

What's in a Name?
New Hampshire Senate Candidate Ethel Doris Haddock legally changed her name to "Granny D," her previous nickname, so that voters would recognize her on the ballot. The feisty 94-year-old needed the name recognition: she was trying to oust the incumbent senator.

Demolition Derby
The event is watched by hundreds of onlookers. The semiannual Orlando Speed World's Crash-a Rama, culminates with more than 12 old school buses speeding their way around a figure-8 racetrack.

Eat Your Art Out

Jim Opasik, a sculptor from Baltimore, Maryland, creates intricate insects, animals, and human figurines from recycled cutlery and everyday kitchen utensils. Among his works of art are a coiled snake made out of overlapping spoons, a wolf spider made from prongs of forks, and an 8 ft (2.4 m) seahorse made of 82 cheese graters and 1,200 spoons, with serving platters for fins and strainers for the snout.

Tread Carefully

A couple in Helena, Montana, have built their home mainly out of tires and aluminum drinks cans. While 250 used car tires form the basic structure of the building, the interior is decorated with more than 13,000 cans. Among the peculiar sculptures is a buffalo made from chicken wire and beer bottles.

What's the Score?

Experimental Chilean artist Antonio Becerro devised a novel way of creating a painting in 2003. Dressed all in white, Becerro stood in front of a huge white canvas "goal" while top soccer player Francisco Huaiquipan took shots with a freshly painted football. Each time Huaiquipan hit the target, the painting received another splash of color.

Take a Gander at this Goose

There's a bird's eye view from every single room of one house in Hazard, Kentucky. For the house, built in the 1940s by John Stacy, is shaped just like a giant goose, with the head and neck protruding from the roof. The home even has egg-shaped windows.

Wishing Well

Royal College of Art student Kate MccGwire created Brood *out of 22,000 chicken wishbones. The piece was displayed as part of her 2004 degree exhibition in London.*

U.S.A.
Alabama

It is illegal to wear a fake moustache that causes laughter in church.

Crazy Golf

Founded by a professional photographer, Douglas Keister, in 1988, Lucifer's Anvil golf course is located right in the heart of Nevada's inhospitable Black Rock Desert. The greens themselves are actually spray-painted on to the course—and they come in a variety of patterns, including a chessboard, a patch of freeway, and even a suburban living-room. Putts often reach 150 yd (140 m) and the players travel around the distance of the course on mountain bikes.

Hippo Crates

Visitors to Hutto, Texas, can't fail to notice that the town is swarming with hippos. There were around 100 at the last count, all arriving in crates on the orders of Mayor Mike Fowler as part of his drive to promote the community. Most of the concrete beasts stand nearly 3 ft (1 m) tall and weigh more than 700 lb (317 kg), but Fowler has plans for a 20 ft (6 m) model—the biggest in the world. The town's fascination with the river horse dates back to the early 20th century, when an escaped circus hippo became their mascot. Hutto has attracted the hippo enthusiasts' society, which is aptly called Hippolotofus. The society's members collect hippo memorabilia, including bracelets, stepping stones, and even the sheet music of a hippo polka. One member proudly drives a hippo-shaped Toyota car.

Backward Looking

Lorrain Chevalier of Philadelphia, Pennsylvania, seen here in 1937, was actually able to sit on her own head! The Chevalier family claims that in 200 years only one person in each generation possessed such dexterity.

Hidden Treasures

In 2003, Corinne Turner of Layton, Utah, bought a 99 cent wallpaper roll at a liquidation store and was stunned to find it hid five paintings by Italian artist Pino Daeni. Turner sold the paintings, which were valued at $6,000 (£3,220), and donated a portion of the revenue to the Multiple Sclerosis Society. Daeni was so inspired by Turner's actions that he contributed 21 more paintings.

Cheaper by the Dozen

When Bob Memmot and Corinne Hanks of Mapleton, Utah, married in June 2003, they significantly increased their family size: together they have a staggering 26 children, ranging in age from 13 to 34—and 34 grandchildren.

Animal Magic

Snowy Farr, of Cambridge, England, is so fond of white mice that he often slips the head of a live one into his mouth! It's all for a good cause though—Snowy has raised more than £60,000 ($111,000) for charity over the past 25 years.

Holy Smoke

Dharmendra Singh of Bikaner, India, chain-smokes—through his ears! Dharmendra, who had always wanted to do something different, can smoke up to 20 cigarettes in a row in this bizarre fashion. He can also whistle through his nose.

Eye of the NeEdLe

Snow White and the Seven Dwarfs.

AN ENGLISH ARTIST is the creator of some minuscule works of art—some of them are even tiny enough to fit inside the eye of a needle!

Willard Wigan, 48, from Birmingham, England, makes his miniature sculptures under a microscope, employing shards of glass to cut his materials and using his own eyelashes as a paintbrush. Each sculpture takes around four months to complete. Among his fantastic works are a model of the Statue of Liberty, so tiny that it fits inside the eye of a needle; Snow White and the Seven Dwarfs, who also sit in the eye of a needle; a golden ship on a speck of crystal; a polar bear standing on a grain of sugar; a mini man wrestling with a life-sized ant;

a re-creation of French sculptor Auguste Rodin's *The Thinker* on a pin head; and a figure of Samson inside a human hair!

An amazing feat— a scene including a house, trees, and greenery carved on the head of a pin!

The Statue of Liberty carved inside the eye of a needle.

15

TOP FIVE
WEIRDEST INJURIES IN BASEBALL

1 **John Smoltz** burned his chest while ironing a shirt that he was wearing

2 **Odiebe McDowell** cut his finger buttering a roll at the Texas Rangers' welcome-home luncheon

3 **Wade Boggs** hurt his back when he lost his balance while trying to put on cowboy boots

4 **Ricky Bones** hurt his lower back getting out of a chair while watching TV in the clubhouse

5 **Kevin Mitchell** strained a muscle while vomiting

Get Stuffed

Chilean artist Caterina Purdy staged an exhibition in Santiago in 2004 in which stuffed animals were transformed into household objects. Artworks included a chick turned into a lamp by wiring a light bulb through its bottom and a "sheep bag"—a lamb carcass with handles.

The Keys to Success

Kurt Meadows of Richlands, Virginia, has been collecting key chains since he was a boy. He now has a massive collection of more than 24,000 key chains—and all of them are different.

All Washed-up

Wayne Snider, of Manassas, Virginia, decided to hold up an armored car as it made its regular pick-up at a local bowling alley. Unfortunately, he mistakenly flashed his gun at the driver of a laundry truck and nabbed a bag of smelly mop heads.

Getting into the Swing

At the Cowboy Cow Pasture Golf Tournament in Springerville, Arizona, cowboys on horseback shoot 18 holes of golf through rough pasture, using cow chips for tees.

An Unusual App-roach

Michael Bohdan believes the humble cockroach to be a work of art. Accordingly, his Combat Cockroach Hall of Fame at Plano, Texas, houses such sights as Roach Perot, which stands on a pile of money; the incomparable Liberoache; and the glamorous Marilyn Monroach, resplendent in white dress and high heels.

Blank Looks

The Old Town House Museum in Cape Town, South Africa, staged an exhibition in 2004 where paintings by 17th century Dutch masters were turned to face the wall! Curator Andrew Lamprecht said: "These are fascinating... to see from behind."

Playing Dirty

There is one soccer tournament in which you can guarantee dirty play. For the Swamp Soccer World Championships are staged on fields so boggy that the players have to plough through hip-deep mud in their exhausting and often fruitless pursuit of the ball. In fact, waders would be more appropriate than soccer boots. Every July, some 250 teams of men and women from all over Europe converge on the tiny Finnish village of Hyrynsalmi, 400 mi (640 km) north of Helsinki. Two halves, each lasting 13 minutes, are played on a field measuring 65 x 38 yd (59 x 35 m). There are six players on each side... and frequent substitutions for tired legs. At the final whistle, the mud-caked participants clean themselves up in an ice-cold lake before heading for a welcome sauna.

Players get down and dirty to compete in Finland's European Swamp Soccer Championships.

Chamber of Horrors

Visitors to an extreme Halloween attraction at Universal Studios in Orlando, Florida, in October 2003 were able to confront their fear of creepy creatures. The brave participants poked their heads into a cage containing scorpions, rats, cockroaches, worms, or snakes! Talk about facing your fears...

Child's Play

An ordinary child's kindergarten painting sold for a staggering $75,000 (£40,000) in 2004, after a crazy bidding war erupted between parents. The colorful abstract of children and animals had been painted by a pre-school class at St. Catherine's School in Melbourne, Australia.

Love is in the Air

Japanese sweethearts Hirotomo Yoshikawa and Tomomi Sato were married in a Tokyo shopping center in 2003—while suspended by a wire 23 ft (7 m) above the ground. Relatives watched the ceremony from a nearby staircase.

A Flying Start

A grandmother from Somerset, England, who had never flown before, took to the skies in 2004 to wing-walk while dressed as a witch. The plane carrying 72-year-old Mattie Williams, reached 100 mph (161 km/h).

The Name of the Game

In 2002, Richard James from St. Albans, England, agreed to change his name to Mr. Yellow-Rat Foxysquirrel Fairydiddle in exchange for a pint of beer. What began as a pub dare ended with Richard paying £38 ($70) to change his name officially. He informed his bank and received a credit card in his strange new name, but when the novelty began to wear off he didn't have enough money to change his name back. He wailed: "I just want to be called Richard again."

On Your Bike!

There's something different about the racing cyclists who turn out for an annual event in Wales. Whereas competitors in the Tour de France wear streamlined outfits designed to make them go faster, these riders are fitted out in snorkels and wetsuits! However, there's a good reason for their strange attire—they're taking part in the World Mountain Bike Bog Snorkelling Championship. The event is held near the town of Llanwrtyd Wells, where a water-filled trench is cut into a peat field. Riders plunge into the water on specially prepared mountain bikes weighed down with lead, and race along two lengths of the bog—approximately 100 yd (90 m)—without using any swimming strokes. Although it's a messy contest, with the cyclists' heads regularly dipping below the surface of the cold, muddy water, the more eccentric riders eschew a wetsuit in favour of a tuxedo and bow tie.

One competitor in the World Mountain Bike Bog Snorkelling Championships rides in style.

Wrong Side of the Tracks

Gene Jackson, of New York, was able to walk along a single rail of a railroad track—on his hands!

Guardian Angel

Jennifer Truman, of Lebanon, New Hampshire, was forced to land her parents' single-engine plane in 2004, despite having no flying experience. After her father passed out, Jennifer contacted an air traffic controller, who talked her safely to the ground.

Fright Wig

Things got hairy recently for passengers flying high on Coney Island's Cyclone roller coaster. A woman's wig flew off, jamming the ride's gears. During the 30 minutes it took for firefighters to untangle the hairpiece, the riders sat perched at the top of a 75-ft (23-m) drop.

Another Toe-nail in His Coffin

When British homeopathic healer Jack Temple died in 2004, as part of his estate he left toenail clippings and hair strands of famous clients including Jerry Hall, Cherie Blair, and the late Princess Diana. The bizarre samples had been pickled in alcohol and stored at his clinic.

Washed Ashore

A very peculiar sight on South Bass Island in Lake Erie, Ohio, is that of an old boat that stands on dry land and is perched on the edge of a cliff. The 220-ton boat was rescued from scrap, and then converted into a family home. It was winched by crane to its present location.

Way to Go!

Florida firm Eternal Ascent Society Inc. offer to send people's ashes into space in order to help families "let their loved ones go." The ashes go up in a biodegradable balloon which, at around 30,000 ft (9,000 m), freezes and then fractures, scattering the ashes into the wind. Their first customer was *Star Trek* fan Celeste Ready of Ocala, Florida, who released her late mother's ashes in a yellow balloon at a park. She said her mother had always wanted to go into space.

Running on Empty

LIFE'S A GAS for Mark Reiff. He has converted his suburban bungalow in Woodland, California, into an authentic, 1950s-style gas station!

One of the pumps out front even offers gas at 11.4 cents per gallon—but don't bother lining up. For, like the other 25 antique pumps, it's just for show. Mark's imagination was fuelled in 1999 when he bought an old gas pump at a yard sale to decorate his house. To emphasize that everything at Reiff's Gas Station is not as it seems, Mark has staged a mock car smash. There are suspicious skid marks on the road, a section of splintered fence, and the rear end of a classic 1956 Oldsmobile impaled in the side of a barn.

A 1956 Oldsmobile sticks out of the barn to give a clue that this is a gas station with a difference.

Full Throttle

For the past 13 years, Al Marcellus has visited more than 30 car races a year, accompanied by the cremated ashes of his best pal, "Wild" Willie Borsch. Borsch loved hot rods—and racing fans love his ashes—which have become a good-luck symbol.

Mark Reiff doesn't really sell fuel from his gas-station home, he just likes "to share fun with other people."

Basket Case

Dave Longaberger wanted an office that immediately told people it was a Longaberger Co. property. Since the company's most popular products are wicker baskets, Longaberger asked architects to design a building in the shape of a giant basket. Like a real Longaberger basket, the seven-story building gets wider as it goes up, so each floor had to be designed independently. The crowning glory of the basket building, which has loomed large over Newark, Ohio, since 1997, is two huge metal handles. Each weighs 75 tons, measures 320 ft (97 m) long (about the length of a soccer field) and is designed to withstand 80 mph (130 km/h) winds.

Architects thought Dave Longaberger was joking when he said he wanted his corporate offices built in the shape of one of the company's trademark baskets. But he had the last laugh in 1997 when 500 employees moved in.

Art and Sole

The most famous building in Bakersfield, California, is Deschwanden's shoe repair shop, because the entire building is shaped like a shoe. Built in 1947, the 30 ft (9 m) long, 20 ft (6 m) high construction dominates the main street. There are a couple of other shoe houses in America, but the Bakersfield shop is the only one complete with laces!

The Last Straw

The whitewashed Pilgrim Holiness Church in Arthur, Nebraska, was built in 1928 out of bales of straw.

IF THE SHOE FITS...

• Before 1800 there were no separately designed shoes for right and left feet

• Toronto's Bata Shoe Museum has over 10,000 shoes, including a pair of Marilyn Monroe's red pumps and a pair of Elton John's platform boots

• Imelda Marcos, former First Lady of the Philippines, had about 3,000 pairs of shoes

• A pair of ruby slippers made for actress Judy Garland to wear in *The Wizard of Oz* (US 1939) sold at auction for $665,000 (£360,500) in 2000

From the Hip

Dutch artist Joanneke Meester made a gun from her own skin in 2004 as a comment on rising violence. Asked why she had surgeons cut a patch of skin from her stomach to cover a plastic gun, she said: "It is easy to shoot someone until you realize it is skin that is being pierced."

Outside Looking In
From the outside it may look like a stylish, mirrored public convenience, but once inside, it takes courage and nerve to use it!

Inside Looking Out
A fully functioning bathroom was unveiled as a public piece of art in 2003. American artist Monica Bonvicini created a minimalist glass cube containing a usable lavatory.

Hitting the Nail on the Head
Francois Russell removes nails that have been hammered into a block of wood—with his teeth.

Floating Home
Helicopter pilot Tim Graves and his family live on the ultimate mobile home. Their house near Ketchikan, Alaska, is a floating ex-logging camp that can be towed anywhere when not held by cables and anchor lines. It is only accessible by boat.

Fluffy Animals
Brazilian artist Tonico Lemos Auad fashions sculptures of squirrels, lions, and cats from bits of fluff he scrapes off carpets.

Toenail Tapestry
In 2004 Uruguayan artist Carlos Capelan put on an exhibition of toenail clippings in Gateshead, England. He claimed that his work "playfully explores issues of self, ego and identity."

Pen Friend
Collecting ball-point pens since childhood, Angelika Unverhau of Dinslaken, Germany, has gathered over 220,000 of them from 146 countries.

Moose on the Loose
You might want to avoid Talkeetna, Alaska, during the town's annual "Moose Dropping Drop" contest, held the second weekend of July. For 32 years, these rowdies have been jumping into a hot-air balloon and dropping numbered pieces of moose dung on to a large "X" target. The winning flinger nabs $1,000 (£540).

Dirty Work
Ben Long, an English artist who draws in the dirt on vans, was shortlisted for a £10,000 ($19,000) art prize in 2002. Unless the vans are washed, his work can last for two months.

A Real Non-event
An antidote to other festivals, the Nothing Festival at Telluride, Colorado, promises no events whatsoever. The festival programme simply announces: "sunrises and sunsets as normal," and that "gravity will continue to be in effect." Visitors are duly thanked for kindly not participating.

Hammering Home his Point
Leo Kongee, of Pittsburgh, known as "the Painless Wonder," could drive 60 penny nails into his nose, without experiencing any discomfort.

Bulldozer Building
The office building of the United Equipment Company alongside freeway 99 in Turlock, California, was designed to look like a giant bulldozer. The boss has his office where the engine should be.

Seeing Double
Geana Morris, of Glenolden, Pennsylvania, has beaten the odds: in August 2004 she gave birth to two sets of identical twins: two boys and two girls. Doctors say the odds of doing so in a quadruplet birth is one in a million. Even more amazing is the fact that Geana is a twin herself, and she delivered the babies on her birthday!

Grains of Truth

This impressive image of the Pope was one of the stunning sculptures made entirely from sand for the 2004 Sand Sculpture Festival on Blankenberge Beach in Belgium.

Ship of Fools

For the Fools' Rules Regatta at Jamestown, Rhode Island, race contestants have two hours to build a sailable boat from non-marine items. One was even built from a Volkswagen car!

Are You Lonesome Tonight?

If you don't have a special honey at home, don't fret: entrepreneur James Wilson has launched "The Amazing Instant Mate" CD. A sultry male or female voice welcomes you home, asks about your day and tells you dinner is ready. The purpose of the CD, says Wilson, is emotional encouragement for the lonely.

Switzerland

It is illegal to flush the toilet after 10 P.M. if you live in an apartment.

Sense of Identity

Scott Ginsberg, of St. Louis, Illinois, has worn a nametag every day since November 2, 2000, just to find out what would happen. He now works with people who want to become more approachable—and says wearing nametags is a great start.

You've Gotta Hand it to Her

This giant sculpture, titled The Legend of Mother Earth, *is made up of thousands of plants. It was one of 60 exhibits from 32 countries in an international exhibition of mosaiculture, or sculpting with plants, in downtown Montréal in August 2003.*

RoLL WiTh the PuNChEs!

AT 50 YEARS OLD, fitness instructor Ken Richmond appeared on the *Ripley's* TV show as the Human Cannon Ball.

His shows of death-defying strength involved having a cannon ball dropped on his head, a wrecking ball smashed into his stomach, and a cannon ball fired at his stomach. He must have a six-pack of steel!

Sparks fly as the gun is fired!

Ken Richmond gathers his strength for the challenge.

Ken tenses before the cannon ball is fired at him.

Smoke billows out and Ken stays tensed and stationary as the ball flies at him!

He begins to double-up as the ball impacts.

Thrown back by the impact and...

...backward he goes into the straw bales!

Urban Space Men
Visitors to Italy could be forgiven for thinking that aliens have landed. Instead, it's simply a home with a twist—a private house in the shape of a spaceship. Take me to your kitchen...

TOP FIVE
UFO SIGHTINGS
1 **Hat-shaped object** (1990), reportedly seen by 10,000,000 people
2 **Oval-shaped object** (1954–2001), 6,500,000 reported sightings
3 **Cigar-shaped object** (1967–98), 1,300,000 reports
4 **Bright, luminous object** (1963–84), 109,000 reports
5 **Formation of lights** (1950), 100,000 reports

Con-duct Unbecoming
Melody Williams of Greers Ferry, Arkansas, has a tacky hobby: making shoes, clothes, jewelry, sculptures, and cards out of duct tape. She has even written a song about her love of it, ending: "may the gray never end."

Sleeping Booty
In April 2004, London's National Portrait Gallery showed an hour-long video of England soccer star David Beckham—sleeping! Artist Sam Taylor-Wood recognized that there was an abundance of action images of the sporting hero and she wanted to focus on a totally original feature of the much-photographed Beckham.

International Date Lines
At London's Nelson's Column in 2004, guest performers took turns reading Japanese artist On Kawara's book that consists solely of 271,000 selected dates between 998,031 BC and AD 1,001,980. The organizers claimed that the passage of time, as depicted in the book, was extremely relevant to our everyday lives.

Food, the Final Frontier
Entrepreneur Andy Gee is building a science-fiction themed restaurant he's calling "Starship Pegasus," 40 mi (64 km) outside Dallas, Texas. Modeled on the spacecraft from *Star Trek: the Next Generation*, the restaurant will feature space-themed dishes and game consoles that will allow diners to interact with players on the Internet. Gee has high hopes for a franchise chain.

Homespun Brew
A German priest has started brewing beer in the most unusual place—his household washing machine. By building a computer interface into the washer so that it could run an automatic brewing programme, Michael Fey from Duisberg, Germany, is able to brew as much as 60 pt (30 l) of the beverage every six weeks.

Chair-lift
Jackie Del Rio was able to lift two tables and six chairs using only his teeth—and as if that wasn't enough, he could also lift a chair with someone on it.

Stupid Parade
St. Stupid is the patron saint of the First Church of the Last Laugh, presided over by the Supreme Pontiff, Bishop Joey. Each April he leads the St. Stupid's Day Parade through the streets of San Francisco, California. The finale is a mass sock fight.

Mystery Man
One night in 1971, D.B. Cooper vanished near Aerial, Washington, with $200,000 (£110,000) in ransom money after hijacking a jet. Since 1974 the town has held an annual D.B. Cooper party, to celebrate his claim to fame. As many as 500 fans gather to remember someone they never knew.

Plenty of Time
More than ten years ago, Edeltraud Dreier from Berlin, Germany, was presented with a kitchen-timer by her daughter. She now has nearly 1,000 different timers, including ones made in Singapore, Japan, U.S.A., and Canada.

A Lot of Bottle
George Plumb used more than 200,000 bottles to recreate some famous landmarks on a 1-acre (0.4-ha) site in British Columbia, Canada. The retired carpenter began in 1962 with a five-room Bottle Castle, soon adding a Taj Mahal and a Leaning Tower of Pisa.

Gimme Shelter
Buses don't come along that often on Unst, the most northerly of Britain's Shetland Islands. Thanks to local schoolboy Bobby Macauley, passengers can wait in one of the world's most luxurious bus shelters—with lace curtains, a comfy sofa, plants, a hot-snacks counter, and a TV set! When the old shelter was knocked down because of a leaking roof, Bobby, then seven years old, petitioned for a new one. Since then local people have donated items for inclusion and Bobby maintains the shelter with a little help from his mom, who bakes the cakes, and a neighbor who waters the plants daily.

Bobby Macauley relaxes, reading a book as he waits for a bus in his customized bus shelter located in the Shetland Islands, Scotland!

Artery Attack

When artist Shihan Hussaini displayed 56 portraits of Jayalalithaa, one of India's leading female politicians, in February 2004, it was an exhibition with a difference. For every portrait was painted in the artist's own blood, drawn from his body with medical assistance over a period of 20 days.

Risky Business

In April 2004, 32-year-old Ashley Revell liquidated all his worldly possessions to gamble the cash on just one single spin of the roulette wheel in Las Vegas, Nevada, as part of the reality TV series *Double or Nothing*. Fortunately for Ashley, Lady Luck was with him: he doubled his money when the ball settled on red number 7, winning him $270,600 (£150,000).

Quackers!

Charlotte Lee of Los Angeles, California, owns more than 1,400 rubber ducks, including vintage ducks, red, pink, and blue ducks—and of course Donald and Daffy.

Feathered Friends

The hills are alive with the sound of quacking when the World Duck Calling Championships come to Stuttgart, Arkansas, every November. Each contestant must perform a hail call, a mating call, a feed call, and a comeback call within 90 seconds. The first national title was claimed back in 1936 by Thomas E. Walsh, one of only two competitors ever to win without the assistance of an artificial duck call. Instead, Walsh relied on creating the duck sounds in the back of his throat.

Top Bill

A staggering 10,000 rubber ducks compete in the annual Great Topeka Duck Race at Lake Shawnee, Kansas.

Hot Spot

The world's tallest thermometer doesn't contain a drop of mercury. It stands 134 ft (40 m) tall in a parking lot at Baker, California, its height marking the hottest-ever temperature in nearby Death Valley—134°F (273°C), back in 1913.

From the Bathtub to the Ocean

In 1992, more than 29,000 rubber ducks accidentally fell off a container ship in the Pacific Ocean. Despite surviving storms, they spent four years trapped in arctic pack ice and then floated on to the Atlantic. Tracked by oceanographer Curt Ebbesmeyer, the ducks now seem to be headed for the west coast of Europe.

Dog and Duck

Bubba the dog underwent surgery to remove a rubber duck from his intestines in Poole, England, in 2004.

Ducks Run Amuck

A man paddles through a sea of plastic ducks during the annual Singapore Duck Race in 2001.

Eat Your Heart Out

Russian Romeo Nikolay Kozlov announced that he was planning to sue his ex-girlfriend for the return of chocolates and other food he had given her. She told the court that she could not return the presents, such as Swiss chocolates, nuts, 6 lb (3 kg) of bananas, and "a bright red apple," because she had already eaten them!

Rat Race

Indian politician Jai Shankar unsuccessfully campaigned for the Indian national elections in 2004, by holding a live rat in his mouth to show support for starving farmers.

To Dial For

An Arkansas football fan was recently held for questioning even though he was completely unaware of what he had done. His cell phone, which was in his back pocket, had automatically called 911—not once but 35 times—as he jumped up and down while cheering, and the police eventually traced the calls and picked him up before he left the stadium.

Where's the Beef?

Don Gorske, from Wisconsin, consumed his 20,000th Big Mac on July 19, 2004. The feat took him 32 years—and he's been eating an average of two Big Macs every day since 1972.

Topsy Turvy

A roller skater was suspended by the steel wheels of one skate attached to a magnet, made by the Dings Magnetic Separator Co. of Milwaukee.

Junk Art

Konstantin Simun, an artist from Boston, Masschusetts, works with one type of material—junk. He uses such items as old tires and traffic cones to create his works of art. He once made a version of Michelangelo's *La Pieta* entirely from cut-up plastic bottles.

A Couple of Swells

Rich "The Locust" LeFevre and his wife, Carlene, are known as the "First Couple" of competitive eating. Carlene is ranked ninth in the world; Rich is ranked fifth. In July 2004, the Nevada couple were placed first and second in the "Swellin' with Melon" contest held in Ohio. Rich downed 11.2 lb (5 kg) of melon, while Carlene managed 9.7 lb (4.3 kg).

To Be or Not To Be

The Woodstock Opera House, in Illinois, is thought to be haunted by the ghost of "Elvira," an actress said to have committed suicide in the theater. Elvira apparently likes seat number 113, and witnesses swear they have seen the seat lower mysteriously. A few even claim to have caught a glimpse of her long, pale hair.

Life on Mars

Hoping some day to walk on the red planet, members of the Mars Society volunteer for two-week stints in secluded habitats, which they hope might simulate the planet's conditions. Always keeping meticulous records, the members wear helmets made from plastic light fixtures and trash-can lids when heading outdoors. The society's 5,000 members, many of whom are NASA employees, are still on the lookout for "a few good Martians" to join them.

Bra-vo!

In January 2001, San Francisco artist Emily Duffy asked friends and family to send her all their old bras. As contributions came in from across the globe, Emily patiently hooked the bras together, end to end, to form a round sculpture known as the "BraBall." By November 2003, the work was complete. It stood 5 ft (1.5 m) tall, weighed 1,800 lb (3,900 kg) and contained no fewer than 18,085 bras, thanks to such generous support.

U.S.A.
Florida

A woman can be fined (only after death) for being electrocuted in a bath-tub because of using self-beautification utensils.

Out of his Tree

Belgian performance artist Benjamin Verdonck chose a weird stage on which to perform his new show in 2004. He was perched in a giant replica of a swallow's nest, 98 ft (30 m) above the ground, on the side of the Anspach Building in Brussels. From this precarious perch, he then tried to conduct conversations with passers-by on the street below.

Patriot Games

Most people have a car parked outside their house, but not a family in Outreau, northern France. Each morning, they open the curtains to be greeted by an enormous bust of former French president, François Mitterand, sculpted from metal and concrete, and covered with grass.

California Dreaming

Architect Eugene Tsui has designed a home for his mother in Berkeley, California, that resembles a fish. The round house even has fin-like structures to dissipate rain.

Letting Rip

In 2004, Ed Charon of Portland, Oregon, reclaimed his crown as the world's greatest ripper of telephone books. The 69-year-old managed to tear through a staggering 39 Portland white-page directories in just three minutes, beating the previous record of 30, which was held by Indiana fitness instructor Mike West.

This ARt is RubBish!

Leo Sewell turns white elephants into priceless art.

LEO SEWELL transforms trash into treasure—and he can sell it for up to $50,000 (£27,000).

All of Sewell's pieces are made from items that he finds in dumpsters and landfills. The Philadelphia-based artist uses old watches, plastic, medals, silverware, and clock parts to fashion life-size sculptures of animals and people. Museums, corporations, and celebrities including Sylvester Stallone collect his work. People who feel strongly about recycling particularly admire his art. "I didn't set out to solve the world's problems with junk," says Sewell, "but I've gotten side benefits from the ecology movement." Lately, Sewell says he's been approached about creating realistic sculptures of people who have passed away, using their possessions.

Ripley's ®
JUNK ART MAN
EXHIBIT NO: 10219
CREATED BY LEO SEWELL, ENTIRELY OUT OF RECYCLED TOYS

Junk has a high price-tag once artist Leo Sewell gets his hands on it. He even makes sculptures of the deceased out of their own possessions.

Ripley's ®
JUNK ART DONKEY
EXHIBIT NO: 10220
LEO SEWELL COLLECTED THE MATERIAL FOR THIS ART FROM PHILADELPHIA STREETS

31

Night Moves

Artist Lyle Estill built a life-size chess set for night games in his backyard. His only regret is that he put it too close to the house: "Some nights when I was lying in bed, I could see torch light flickering on the ceiling because players had shown up for a game without me."

Presidential Pets

After secretly collecting samples of fur from the Reagans' dog, Lucky, Claire McLean became so fascinated with the history of White House pets that she founded the Presidential Pet Museum in Lothian, Maryland. More than 1,500 items relate to such diverse creatures as Calvin Coolidge's racoons, an alligator presented to John Quincy Adams, and the Kennedy children's hamsters.

Short, back, and upside-down!

Customers who are willing to pay that little bit extra—and risk their necks—can pay a visit to Senol Demir, a barber in Adapazari, Turkey, who offers an upside-down shave as part of the service!

JOIN THE CLUB

• After missing two short putts in 1919, former US Open champion Chick Evans angrily holed out with the handle of his umbrella

• Canadian golfer Moe Norman once used a Coca-Cola bottle as a tee in the Los Angeles Open

• Playing in Maryland in 1979, Dr. Sherman A. Thomas was so distracted by the honking of a Canada goose that he killed it with a blow to the head and was fined $500 (£270) for killing a goose out of season

Soda Mountain

Brazilian bar owner Celio de Oliveira has built a house using only empty plastic soda bottles. He started collecting the discarded bottles to clean up Mage Beach in Rio de Janeiro and, after building a bottle wall at his bar, decided to use the remaining 10,000 to construct a small house. He said: "The house will last forever and if it caught fire, we would just throw sand on it."

Body Art

Two Chilean artists opened an exhibition of artwork in 2003—made from human body parts. Carmen Ariztia and Francisca Aninat's pieces included hairbrushes made out of hair and crosses made out of bones and teeth.

Lights On, Nobody Home

In 2001, English artist Martin Creed won the prestigious Turner Prize and £20,000 ($39,000) for a piece of work entitled *The Lights Going On and Off*—which consisted simply of an empty gallery and a pair of flashing lights. His previous works have included crumpled balls of paper and sticky-tac sculptures.

A Fridge Too Far

Ex-Royal Marine Paul McKelvey climbed the 3,560 ft (1,085 m) Mount Snowdon in 20 days—with a full-sized refrigerator strapped to his back. Beginning from his home in Liverpool, England, Paul completed the 100-mi (161-km) charity trek to the summit of the Welsh mountain in four days. Although he removed the shelves and the motor, the fridge still weighed around 88 lb (40 kg). He said: "It started off as a joke, but then I decided to give it a go."

Fungi Fun

Visitors to Charlevoix, Michigan, could be forgiven for thinking that they have wandered into an enchanted forest. In the 1950s, Earl Young built an estate of homes with a difference—they all look like mushrooms.

Snake Charmer

Liu Lang, China's infamous "snake man," has mastered some bizarre skills. He can lift a bucket of water using his eyeballs, swallow steel bearings and then spurt them from his mouth, eyes, nose, or ears, and lead a snake in through his nostril and out through his mouth.

That Really Takes the Biscuit

John Dobbins of Glendora, New Jersey, lives in a three-story house that is shaped like a cookie jar!

It's a Steal

German artist Gerhard Zerbes announced that he did not want the public to buy pictures from his 2003 exhibition—he wanted people to steal them! Zerbes said the bizarre arrangement was intended to test human creativity and ingenuity in the face of surveillance cameras.

Feline Groovy

Humans take second place in the San Diego home of artists Frances Mooney and Bob Walker, because the house is designed as a luxury hotel for their cats. There is a cat gym, a 7 ft (2 m) scratching post, and 110 ft (33 m) of cat paths. Apart from the inevitable cat motifs, the décor is purple and pink—because cats apparently like those colors.

Wheels of Fortune

Sculptor Ptolemy Allerington from Brighton, England, creates works of art from discarded auto hubcaps. He turns them into sharks, piranhas, and other fish and sells them for up to £1,500 ($1,800) each.

U.S.A.
Arizona

It is illegal for men and women over the age of 18 to have less than one missing tooth visible when smiling.

WISH UPON A STAR

• When the Stars and Stripes flag is flown upside-down, it is recognized as a call for help

• An old English drinking song provided the music for "The Star-spangled Banner"

• Lawyer Francis Scott Key wrote the words to "The Star-spangled Banner" on the back of an envelope in 1814

• In 2002, the Floral Flag, depicting the Stars and Stripes, measured 740 ft (225 m) long and 390 ft (120 m) wide. It contained over 400,000 larkspur plants, which produced two million flowers

Jump on the Bandwagon
The VW Bug that Harrod Blank calls "Pico De Gallo," is covered in records and working instruments, it is a tribute to rock 'n' roll. Harrod Blank, an art car photographer, has created many art cars of his own.

Having a Whale of a Time
In the 1950s, Eero Saarinen designed Ingalls Hockey Rink at Yale University in New Haven, Connecticut, in the shape of a whale! The "dorsal fin" undulates into the roof and beneath its black "nose," the whale's "mouth" opens to welcome 3,000 spectators.

The Best Possible Taste
James Whistler, the famous American artist, once dyed his rice pudding green so that it didn't clash with the walls of his dining room!

Stretch Limbo
In 2003, Chilean artist Sebastian Mahaluf staged an exhibition consisting of an otherwise empty room, which he filled with more than 200 elastic bands stretched from wall to wall. Visitors were forced to turn themselves into contortionists in order to cross the room and reach the rest of Santiago's Balmaceda gallery.

Hat Tricks
The Red Hat Society, primarily for women over 50 who meet to celebrate middle age, has become a cultural phenomenon. It was founded just six years ago with 18 members, and there are now 33,000 chapters with 750,000 members across the U.S.A. These fun-loving gals are easily identified by their red hats, purple clothing, and huge smiles.

Car Crazy
Auto-mad architect Dan Scully has built his New Hampshire home in the shape of a car. It has two round windows as headlights and even the bumper from a Volkswagen bus. The theme is continued inside, where old car seats provide the furniture and the bathroom tiles mimic tire tread!

Potty Pictures
Virginia Williams of Providence, Rhode Island, is captivated by photographs of toilets and has more than 100 in her collection.

PANDAMONIUM

Among the weird and wonderful machines in the 2004 Kinetic Sculpture Race was Pandamonium, powered by two cuddly kinetinauts.

I N 1969, HOBART BROWN and four other artists pioneered the first Kinetic Sculpture Race down Main Street in Ferndale, California.

Today the wacky races, which involve moving sculptures, have spread to Oregon, Maryland, Washington, and even as far as Australia, but the 42-mi (68-km) cross-country challenge from Great Arcata to Ferndale remains the one they all want to win.

On Top of the World

American sailor Alvin "Shipwreck" Kelly spent more than 20,000 hours of his life sitting on top of flagpoles as part of a craze during the 1920s. He once sat for 49 consecutive days atop a pole in Atlantic City.

Shark Attack

Since 1986, the strangest house exterior in Britain has been a terraced home in Oxford owned by American Bill Heine. Heine's house has a 25 ft (7.6 m) fiberglass sculpture of a shark buried nose-down in the roof—a symbol, he claims, of man's inhumanity.

A Shining Example

Before his death in 2002, Dr. Hugh Hicks, a dentist from Baltimore, Maryland, collected more than 75,000 light bulbs from all around the world.

The Quiet Man

Jim Sulkers of Manitoba, Canada, led such a reclusive life that when he died at home in 2002 at the early age of just 52, it was another two years before his mummified body was eventually discovered by the police. In all that time, not one of the neighbors had noticed that he wasn't around.

Pillow Talk

The folk of Kenwood, California, have a unique way of celebrating Independence Day—with the World Pillow Fighting Championships. Competitors, who straddle a slippery pole while holding a wet feather pillow, must knock their opponent off the pole using only the pillow. Kicking is forbidden and contestants must swing their pillow at least once every 30 seconds to avoid disqualification.

Up, Up, and Away

Ever since seeing a movie in which a boy floated away on a string of balloons, Englishman Ian Ashpole had dreamed of emulating the feat. In 2001, the 46-year-old achieved his goal by filling 600 toy balloons with helium and sailing to a height of 11,000 ft (3,353 m) over the Cambridgeshire countryside. When the balloons started popping due to the extreme altitude, he cut himself free with a knife and parachuted safely to the ground.

Homes from Home

Despite being more than 8,000 mi (12,870 km) from Germany, the town of Leavenworth, Washington State, was reborn in the 1960s as a Bavarian themed village. Authentic Bavarian shops sell wooden clocks and there is a Great Bavarian Ice Festival in January, conducted to the sound of alpine horns.

Bird Fancier

Linda Briggs from Gloucestershire, England, has amassed more than 1,500 toy penguins. Her husband Tom also became part of the collection when he had images of penguins tattooed on his arms and chest.

Inflation Proof

Inflation holds no fears for Bilby Wallace, which is just as well because the former astronaut lives in an inflated house. The residence, situated in the Rockies and designed by architect Jonathan Zimmerman, is built around an inflated balloon. To help anchor the reinforced nylon walls, the rear of the house is 12 ft (4 m) underground.

A Riot of Color

Visitors take a shine to Jean Linard's house—for the artist has created a bright ceramic façade to his home at Neuvy Deux Clochers, France. He built the entire house himself over 40 years, with materials from ruined buildings. "Each time I had another child I added another room," explains Jean, and since he has eight children, the house grew and grew. Strange metallic creatures with heads made of wine bottles line the drive and the roof is decorated with red, blue, and yellow tiles that Jean fired himself. There is even a bright ceramic pool, crossed by stepping stones, and a multi-colored "cathedral," complete with a nave.

French artist Jean Linard built his own home and covered it in multi-colored ceramic tiles.

A Real Tongue Lashing
In 1938, Leona Young, of New York, known as "the Devil's Daughter," used a regulation plumber's torch to pass flames over her tongue.

U.S.A.
Ohio
Women are forbidden from wearing patent leather shoes, lest men see reflections of their underwear.

Nice to Meat You
Chilean artist Alejandro Prieto opened a new exhibition in 2004, in which all her works were made out of meat! One piece was a recreation of a scene from *Little Red Riding Hood* in which the wolf, whose ears were made from bacon, was hiding under bed covers made from ham.

Taking the Plunge
Every New Year's Day, some 300 tuxedo-clad swimmers dive into the icy waters of Mackerel Cove, Rhode Island, for the Penguin Plunge.

Cave Dwelling
Fearing Armageddon, millionaire John Hay bought land near Parthenon, Arkansas, in the 1960s and developed a luxury bomb shelter in a cave. Now a private dwelling, it has a natural waterfall in the lounge.

Wrap Artist
In 2003, British sculptor Antony Gormley wrapped 240 nude models in saran wrap and made plaster casts of their bodies. He had more than 1,000 volunteers ranging in age from five to 95.

It's in the Can
A scaled down replica of St. Peter's Basilica was constructed in Rome from 10 million used aluminum cans.

37

GrEat BaLL of PaiNT

Mike Carmichael accepts requests from total strangers to have a layer of the ball painted in their honor. He often paints their name or message on the ball.

EVERY DAY SINCE 1977, house painter Mike Carmichael of Alexandria, Indiana, has applied at least one coat of paint to a regulation baseball.

More than 17,000 coats of paint later, the initial 9-in (22-cm) circumference has ballooned to more than 104 in (264 cm), and the weight of the ball has increased to 1,100 lb (500 kg) making it the world's largest ball of paint. Mike lets a guest of honor paint every hundredth coat, and has kept detailed records of the many colors of the ball's layers. The ball has now grown so big that he has had to build a special room in his house just to store it. The attraction has drawn many visitors, some from as far away as Thailand.

Twine Passions

Francis A. Johnson's efforts (top right) inspired Frank Stoeber of Cawker City, Kansas, who managed to roll over 1,600,000 ft (487,680 m) of twine into a sphere 11 ft (3 m) in diameter. But just when he seemed certain to overtake his Darwin rival, Stoeber died. The Cawker City ball then became a community project, but Johnson's supporters dismiss its superiority because it became the work of more than one man.

Close to the Wire

"Clonia," created by Lyle Lynch of Phoenix, Arizona, was the biggest barbed-wire ball in the world from 1970 until the late 1990s. With a diameter of 80 in (2 m) and a weight of more than 5,000 lb (2,268 kg), it consists of 16 mi (26 km) of wire!

Stringing us Along

For years Francis A. Johnson spent his lunch hour painstakingly wrapping twine on his farm in Darwin, Minnesota. When he died in 1989, the ball measured 12 ft (4 m) in diameter and weighed 17,400 lb (7,892 kg).

Let's Stick Together

Boys Town, Nebraska, is home to the world's largest ball of stamps. The ball, which weighs in at 600 lb (272 kg), is housed in the town's Philamatic Museum. It was pasted together by the local stamp-collecting club over the course of six months in the early 1950s. Why did the philatelists get so stuck in? "It must have been an exceptionally cold winter," says the museum's director.

First-class Effort

In the 1930s, postmaster Virden Graham of Indiana completed a 130-lb (59-kg) ball of brown cotton string that he had taken from first-class bundles. It took him 16 years, and the ball consisted of an impressive 78 mi (126 km) of string.

Ball Room

Weighing more than 6 tons and measuring 41 in (104 cm) wide, this ball was created by J.C. Payne of Texas to beat the previous world's biggest ball of binder twine, the Darwin Ball.

Ripley's®
GIANT BALL OF TWINE
EXHIBIT NO: 10787
THIS GIANT BALL OF TWINE MEASURES
42 IN (107 CM) IN CIRCUMFERENCE

To Cap it All

Over a period of 30 years, Emanuele "Litto" Damonte (1892–1985), the "Hubcap King" of Pope Valley, California, collected more than 2,000 vehicle hubcaps.

Hubcap in Hand

Known as the "Hubcap Queen," Lucy Pearson of the U.S. has a collection of more than 200,000 hubcaps!

Foul Play

Eighty-three-year-old Abe Coleman of Tacoma, Washington, has a penchant for catching foul balls. For the past two decades, the sprightly octogenarian has stood in the parking lot of the town's minor-league ballpark during every game, complete with baseball glove in hand, running back and forth in hot pursuit of all those errant baseballs. When one really goes astray, he has even been known to crawl under parked cars to retrieve it.

That's a Record

In the 1960s and 1970s, a Washington, D.C. man known as "Mingering Mike" created fake long-playing records. Each album, complete with a hand-illustrated cover, full liner notes, lyric sheets, a bar code, and even a cardboard "record," was designed with painstaking detail—some of them were even shrink-wrapped! Thirty-eight of the convincing fakes were discovered at a flea market as recently as 2004.

TOP FIVE
MOST COMMON OBSESSIONS

1 Fear of contamination
2 Fear of causing harm to someone else
3 Fear of making mistakes
4 Fear of behaving in a way that is socially unacceptable
5 Need for exactness

If the Hubcap Fits...

Sculptor Ptolemy Elrington of Brighton, England, recycles old hubcaps into sculptures, mostly of fish, "to try to say things about our wasteful society."

Split Personality

England's Alfred West holds the world record for splitting hairs: he split a human hair into 18 parts, making all the cuts from one point.

Habit Forming

Statistics compiled by the Obsessive Compulsive Foundation suggest that as many as one in 50 adults in the United States suffers from Obsessive Compulsive Disorder. These sufferers become obsessed by doubts or worries to the point where their lives become disrupted. They often feel compelled to perform certain actions—for example, repeated hand-washing, arranging, counting, collecting, and hoarding—in order to alleviate their distress.

The Little Top

Roll up for the smallest show on earth! Paul Tandy from Warwick, England, has spent the last nine years creating a model circus, with miniature animals, and more than 500 entertainers. Inspired by a visit to the circus when Paul was ten, P.J. Tandy's International Circus is accurate in every detail, down to a cannon, which fires a mini human cannon ball, and tiny elephant droppings.

Stub it Out

Since 2001, anti-smoking activist Zhang Yue has attempted to convert China's 4 million smokers—one by one. Traveling around the country, he approaches smokers and tries to convince them to quit. He will even buy their cigarettes from them.

Swat Team

After a fly wrecked a lucrative deal by landing in a client's meal, Chinese businessman Hu Xilin vowed revenge. That was ten years ago, and since then Hu says that he has killed 88 lb (40 kg) of flies and can identify 25 different species.

On the House

When John F. Kennedy was still president, John Zweifel decided to build a miniature version of the White House. Forty years later, the 60 ft (18 m) by 20 ft (6 m) replica has a place of honor at Zweifel's House of Presidents in Clermont, Florida. On a scale of one inch to one foot, the model mirrors the real thing right down to cracks in the walls and coffee stains on the rugs. There are lights in every room, the toilets flush, and there is even a tiny working TV in the West Wing. John sees only one problem with his fiddly miniature White House: "If a light goes out on a chandelier, it could take more than 16 hours to change it."

Chinese Tea

Twelfth-century Chinese Emperor Hui Tsung drank tea, wrote about tea, held tea-identifying competitions, and had teahouses built. His tea obsession was so great that he hardly noticed when his empire was overthrown by the Monguls.

Open House

Joseph Peterson of Cloquet, Minnesota, collects presidential and first lady memorabilia. His filing cabinets, full of material, include Christmas cards from the White House, and pictures of presidential dogs. He has shaken hands with every president since Gerald Ford, apart from Ronald Reagan.

Dish the Dirt

Glenn Johanson collects dirt from all around the world and proudly displays it in glass vials in his Museum of Dirt in Boston.

Barefaced Cheeks

In January 2004, British rambler Stephen Gould achieved his ambition of completing a 1,000-mi (1,600-km) walk—naked. He was arrested several times along the way and served two jail sentences.

Totally Nuts

Elizabeth Tashjian is nuts about nuts. Known as "The Nut Lady," Elizabeth, an accomplished artist, has been fascinated with the fruit since she thought she saw a human face in a Brazil nut in 1938. She then opened a Nut Museum in Old Lyme, Connecticut, and even performed a song about nuts on *The Tonight Show Starring Johnny Carson*. Until it closed in 2002, the museum housed all manner of nutty artifacts—nutcrackers, nut masks, nut sculptures, and the world's largest nut, a 35-pounder from the Seychelles.

The Name of the Game

A massive fan of the games console, John Sterling actually changed his name by law to Sony PlayStation!

Cartoon Capers

GEORGE C. REIGER JR., a Pennsylvania postal worker, is goofy about Disney characters.

The 51-year-old has more than 1,650 Disney tattoos from the base of his neck to the tops of his toes. His first cartoon tattoo was Mickey Mouse on his forearm. Now the whale from *Pinocchio* (US 1940) yawns on his belly, Beauty and the Beast dance on his left shoulder, and Alice in Wonderland fills his upper arm. On his back are 103 Dalmatians—his tattoo artist got carried away!

George spends $50,000 (£27,000) a year on his Disney habit and has even spent all six of his honeymoons at Disney World in Florida.

George Reiger also owns more than 19,500 Disney collectibles and lives in a custom-built, Disney-themed house.

Taking the Mickey

Benji Breitbart, 22, is so mad about all things Disney that he spends six days a week at Disneyland, California. He knows the entire history of the park, dresses almost exclusively in Disney clothes, and refers to Disney as "we" even though he doesn't work for the corporation.

All Mixed Up
An Englishman who gave up trainspotting as it was too boring now has more than 1,000 pictures of cement-mixers. Ronnie Crossland, of Yorkshire, first developed his passion after spotting a new mixer being delivered to a building site in 1987. He has since traveled more than 200,000 mi (322,000 km) taking photos of cement-mixers, which he describes as "things of incredible beauty."

Skater Mom
Barbara Odanaka can't seem to outgrow her childhood preoccupation with skateboarding. When she isn't skating around her house in Orange County, California, she is busy running the International Society of Skateboarding Moms, or using her skateboard to distribute books to needy children, or promoting her book, which is titled... you guessed it, *Skateboard Mom*.

Get Set, Go
Jane Withers, a child star of Hollywood films of the 1930s and 1940s, has a collection of showbiz memorabilia large enough to fill a warehouse. Her stash of more than 42,000 items includes parts of TV and movie sets, costumes, dolls, and scripts.

Praise the Gourd
Marvin Johnson could never get enough gourds. He and his wife Mary had so many of the strange-looking vegetables at their house in Angier, North Carolina, that they set up a Gourd Museum in 1965. The exhibits are mostly of gourd art. There is a gourd xylophone, a gourd Popeye, and a menagerie of gourd animals. "I've made lots of friends through gourds," Marvin once said.

The Best Possible Paste
Dr. Valkopolkov of Saginaw, Michigan, has collected more than 800 tubes of toothpaste from around the world, including such exotic flavors as tuna and Scotch.

Double-blind Test
Frank Keith of Illinois, could write backward, upside-down, and blind-folded! He could also simultaneously write any name or phrase with his left hand in front and his right hand behind.

The Write Stuff
Zelma George, of Canton, Ohio, had an amazing ability—not only could she write both forward and backward, she could also write upside down and upside down backward!

The Hole Story
The world's most pierced woman, Brazilian Elaine Davidson, puts her finger through her pierced tongue! So far she has 1,903 body piercings. Elaine has also been known to walk on beds of fire, broken glass, and nails. For her next feat: she wants to exceed 2,000 piercings!

Is it a Bird, Is it a Plane...

Native Californian John Ninomiya is one of only a few cluster balloonists in the world. He and his crew tie between 50 and 150 latex balloons on to a harness... and up and away he goes. So far, he has made about two dozen flights.

Duck and Cover

Nancy Townsend is so obsessed with her pet ducks and geese that she has invented diapers for them so that they can live indoors. Nancy dresses as Mother Goose, and is often seen taking her birds for walks on a leash.

Mac Attack

Computer technician Andrew Dusing makes furniture out of old Macintosh computer boxes and their Styrofoam inserts. His New York apartment is furnished with his recycled creations: a sofa, a dining table, a set of chairs, and CD racks. His ambition is to one day make a '57 Chevy.

Hearse Case Scenario

Rachel Ellam-Lloyd was so obsessed with vampires that she used to drive her young daughter to school in London in a 23-ft (7-m) long hearse. Little Georgina sat in the back where the coffin should be. Rachel also used the hearse—bought for her by her husband—to go shopping and to attend meetings of the Vampire Connections group.

A Sick Sense of Humor

Steve Dixon has been collecting airline sick-bags for 23 years. In that time he has amassed a collection of more than 180 bags.

Blood Brothers

Grab a bite with local vampires on International Vampire Meetup Day. Once a month, thousands of aspiring bloodsuckers meet at an appointed time in more than 650 different locations around the world. The most popular cities for meetups: London, followed by New York City, and Houston, Texas.

BeAM ME UP?

STAR TREK FANS Mikel and Craig Salsgiver displayed the Vulcan greeting as they renewed their marriage vows on the Starship Enterprise.

Who would have Guest?

Miosav Static has attended more than 1,500 weddings in western Serbia… without ever being invited! Miosav, who finds out the times and locations from the local media, says he loves the atmosphere and food at weddings. He doesn't expect something for nothing, however, and always takes a present for the bride.

The Salsgivers were among four couples to be selected to take part in the "Intergalactic Weddings" package, offered by the Las Vegas Hilton's "*Startrek*: The Experience" attraction. The vows, which were taken on the couple's fifth wedding anniversary, were taken on the bridge of the *Starship Enterprise*.

TOP FIVE
SPACED OUT

1 **Orlando, Florida, dentist Denis Bourguignon** and his entire staff wear *Star Trek* uniforms while working on patients

2 **Britain's David Nutley** is so obsessed with *Star Wars* that he's made his own version. He filmed *Dark Skies* in his spare room and nearby woods for $900 (£500)

3 ***Star Trek* fan Barbara Adams** of Little Rock, Arkansas, wears her Starfleet Commanding Officer's uniform everywhere she goes —even on jury duty

4 **British Trekkie Tony Alleyne** has turned his flat into a replica of the Starship Enterprise

5 ***Star Trek* fan Daryl Frazetti** from Boston, Massachusetts, dressed his cat Bones in a Dr. McCoy uniform

Mikel Salsgiver made all the outfits for her Trekkie wedding party.

Holy Roller

"Rolling saint" Lotan Baba makes holy pilgrimages through the Indian countryside by lying on the ground and rolling sideways to his destination. In 1995, he rolled nearly 2,500 mi (4,023 km), averaging between 6 mi (10 km) and 13 mi (21 km) a day. He embarked on a 1,500-mi (2,414-km) roll from India to Pakistan in 2003.

"Rolling Saint" Lotan Baba on a roll in 1994 for world peace, which ended, appropriately, at the Peace Pagoda in Battersea Park, London, England.

Log Jam

The front yards of Bynum, North Carolina, are adorned with wooden figures of dogs, elephants, giraffes, and other animals. They are the work of Clyde Jones who, for more than 20 years, has used his chainsaw to carve out distinctive critters from log stumps. Dozens of his creations stand outside his own house, which was covered in penguins.

ART MADE OUT OF LINT
EXHIBIT NO: 13998
THIS LINT ARTWORK OF JOHN WAYNE IS ACTUALLY LIFE-SIZE, AT 6 FT, 4 IN (2 M)

Fowl Play

Armando Parra is a professional chicken-catcher in Key West, Florida, where an estimated 2,000 of the fast-breeding birds run loose in the streets. Armando catches the chickens unharmed, and then they are sent to live on a farm.

How the West was Washed

Slater Barron of Long Beach, California, collects lint from her own laundry, and from that of neighbors and friends, and stores it in color-coded boxes in her studio/garage. She then uses the lint to make pictures of all kinds of people and objects, including this portrait of actor John Wayne, which can be seen in the Ripley's Museum in Hollywood.

U.S.A.
Iowa

One-armed piano players must perform for free.

Royal Flush
Australian Janet Williams is such a fan of the British monarchy that she has "royalty rooms" in her home in Sydney, dedicated to her collection of royal memorabilia.

The Winner by a Nose
Ashrita Furman of New York holds the most world records of any individual, including titles for pogo-stick jumping, brick-carrying, underwater rope-jumping, and sack-racing. In New York in 2004, he also succeeded in pushing an orange for 1 mi (1.6 km) in a time of 24 minutes, 36 seconds, using only his nose!

Slap Dash
After years of frustration at finding grammatical errors in newspapers, Jeff Rubin, who runs a newsletter production business, created a new holiday: National Punctuation Day. He hopes that the holiday, which is celebrated every year on August 22, will bring some attention to the widespread problem of poor punctuation.

Full of Beans
In the 1990s, Peggy Gallagher left her job as a paralegal in Chicago to pursue her obsession with Beanie Baby toys. She tracked down rare ones, wrote a book about them, and became a Beanie Baby authenticator—someone who decides if Beanies are genuine.

Grand Slam
Jason Alan Pfaff of Ohio is a man on a mission: to visit every single Denny's restaurant in the world. His website contains reviews of the 200 or more locations he has visited.

The School Run

Author and athlete Siri Chinmoy sponsored a curious endurance race in New York City in 1998. The 3,100-mi (4,989-km) course consisted of running round and round a Queens school between 6 a.m. and midnight for weeks on end. The leading runners completed some 115 laps of the school each day. The winner, Hungary's Istvan Sipos, finished the course in 47 days.

Surf's Up

On February 29, 1976, Dale Webster pledged to surf off the coast of California every day until Leap Day fell again on the fifth Sunday of February. That meant 28 years, or more than 10,000 days of surfing, before he stopped in 2004. He postponed his wedding for ten years, never took a vacation, and took poorly-paid night jobs so that he would be free for surfing.

Stuck on You

Art student Jillian Logue, of Florida, made this senior prom dress and tuxedo entirely out of colored duct tape!

Wash Day Blues?

No stranger to the Ripley's Believe It or Not! television show, Kevin Thackwell, has broken records by attaching 120 clothes pins to his face and neck. Kevin, who is also known as the "Clothes Pin Man," clearly isn't worried about wrinkles.

Casket Case

Casket carver Mark Zeabin from Krestova, British Columbia, makes a line of furniture that will last a lifetime—and then some. For Mark is so keen on coffins that he has designed stereo stands, bars, and even sofa beds that will convert into coffins upon the owner's demise. His theory is that it's a false economy to buy a bookshelf that stores only books when you can have one that will eventually store you too.

Reverse Gear

India's Samir Tandon can sing songs, read newspapers, and repeat entire conversations backward.

Don't Look Back

During the 1930s, Plennie Wingo walked backward around the world! Later he walked backward from LA to San Francisco as part of a Ripley's museum promotion. He always wore mirrored glasses so he could see where he was going.

Tomb Raider

Sara Lock from Suffolk, England, was so enthralled by ancient Egyptian culture that she turned her spare room into an Egyptian tomb.

Completely Cuckoo

With 561 cuckoo-clocks, Roman Piekarski, proprietor of the Cuckooland Museum in Cheshire, England, has the largest collection of cuckoo-clocks in the world. He dreads Daylight Saving Time, for twice a year it takes him around 12 hours to change all his clocks!

White Spirit

In November 2003, 80-year-old Paul Schipper clocked up 3,697 consecutive days' skiing on Sugarloaf mountain in Maine, despite the face that he is almost blind in one eye. Since 1981, the senior citizen has been out skiing every single day that the mountain has been open.

CHRISTMAS CRACKERS!

SOME FOLK WISH it could be Christmas every day—and for Andy Park it is! Since 1991, Andy, of Wiltshire, England, has been celebrating Christmas on a daily basis.

Andy Park must confuse many people by dressing as "Mr. Christmas" all year round— but he's never short of tinsel to wear.

Every single day, Andy watches the Queen's speech and treats himself to a huge Christmas feast. He calculated that his annual intake is 5,450 turkeys, 18,250 roast potatoes, 43,800 Brussels sprouts, 1,825 turnips,

Faux Fir Tree
Car junk yards are rarely known as scenes of great beauty, but this one in Hamburg, Germany, made an effort to get into the festive spirit for Christmas 2003 by piling its scrap vehicles into the shape of a giant, rusty Christmas tree.

3,650 parsnips, 1,825 pots of cranberry sauce, 7,300 gravy cubes, 7,360 mince pies, and 2,350 Christmas puddings. This is washed down with 8,000 glasses of sherry and 1,560 bottles of champagne. He has also bought 30 artificial trees, 10,000 balloons, and 33,000 ft (10,058 m) of tinsel. He estimates that his festive fetish has cost him more than £100,000 ($185,000)... not to mention a seriously expanding waistline.

Santa's Little Helpers

Alex Adlam has no shortage of helpers when it comes to preparing Christmas lunch. For his house in Cheltenham, England, is full of hundreds of Santas in all shapes and sizes. Alex is unable to resist any item of Christmas memorabilia, from snowmen and reindeer, to stockings and elves.

His collection of ornaments, plates, cushions, and decorations has turned his home into a grotto. It comes as no surprise that Alex likes to dress for the part, donning a white beard and Santa suit to fit in with his festive surroundings.

Ho, ho, ho! Alex Adlam proudly displays his vast collection of Christmas memorabilia.

TOP FIVE CELEBRITY PHOBIAS

1 **Madonna**
brontophobia
a fear of thunder

2 **Sid Caesar**
tonsurphobia
a fear of haircuts

3 **Sigmund Freud**
siderodromophobia
a fear of train travel

4 **John Cheever**
gephyrophobia
fear of crossing bridges

5 **Natalie Wood**
hydrophobia
a fear of water
(she died by drowning)

In a Spin
In April 2004, hula hoop performer Alesya Goulevich spun 100 hula hoops simultaneously, at the Big Apple Circus, Boston.

Living Doll
A Maryland couple have raised a Cabbage Patch doll as their only son for 19 years. Pat and Joe Posey treat the 1 ft (0.3 m) doll, christened Kevin, as a human. He "speaks" through Joe, has his own 1,000 sq ft (93 sq m) playroom at the couple's home, a full wardrobe and $4,000 (£2,200) of savings for when he goes to college!

Going For a Thong
Since 1996, Russell Doig has gathered over 4,000 thongs from his local beach near Townsville, Queensland, Australia. Doig combs Alva beach every weekend, scooping up washed-up thongs with a special spike before nailing them to his back fence.

Queen Nefertiti
Forty-year-old schoolteacher Elizabeth Christensen is obsessed with looking like the ancient Egyptian Queen Nefertiti! She has paid over $250,000 for more than 240 operations to change her face to look like a famous ceramic sculpture of the queen.

She Ain't Heavy

An Indian man is carrying his elderly mother on a 17-year-long pilgrimage from their home in northern India to Bangalore in the south. Kailashgiri Brahmachari carries his blind mother in a basket on one shoulder and in another basket, their belongings. By walking a couple of miles each day, he hopes to reach their destination in 2013.

Big Breakfast

Frank Staley has collected over 400 breakfast cereal boxes. This is 400 too many for his wife, who has ordered him to move some of them out of their home in Ohio.

Captain Cutlass

As his alter ego, Captain Cutlass, Adrian Collins, who is 36 and from Kent, England, organizes and competes in the annual World Plank Walking Championship, held on the Isle of Sheppey. Plankers come from all over the world to take part.

Watching You

During one series of TV's *Big Brother*, Gillian Dutfield of Shropshire, England, lived her life according to the housemates. She cooked the same meals as them, and ate and slept at the same time as them. She even shaved her pet dog with the message to the audience, "Vote for Brian!"

Gnome Home

More than 2,000 garden gnomes and pixies roam free at Ann Atkin's gnome sanctuary in Devon, England. Ann, who is 67, founded the International Gnome Club in 1978. She stoutly defends her lengthy garden gnome fixation by saying, "I think people form an affinity with them."

Buttery Burial

In "The Popcorn Sarcophagus," the renowned competitive eater, Crazy Legs Conti, was buried alive under 100 cu ft (3 cu m) of popcorn. Breathing through a custom fitted snorkel as he ate, he used colored lights to signal—red meant "danger," green meant "OK," and yellow meant "alert, need more butter!"

Soil Baron

This U.S. soil collector gathered soil from every single U.S. state. He kept each sample in a small container attached to a map on the spot where it came from.

He's a Barbie Boy

Tony Mattia of Brighton, England, owns more than 1,100 Barbie dolls. He started collecting them in the 1960s. "My parents bought me an Action Man," he says, "but I dressed him up in Barbie's clothes." A Barbie that he bought for £1 ($2) in 1962 is now worth at least £200 ($370). Tony changes the costume of every doll once a month.

Bottle Neck

Indian artist Mayapandi has been painting figures on the inside of bottles for the past six years and hopes eventually to fit 500 in one bottle.

Running on Empties

David Pimm has a collection of more than 10,000 different milk bottles at his home on the Isle of Wight, England.

Navel Gazing

Every day since 1984, Graham Barker from Perth, Australia, has been collecting fluff from his navel. He now has 0.54 oz (16.8 g)—the world's largest collection.

In For a Penny...

Arizona's Steve Baker is crazy about pennies. He makes skirts, shirts, and bathing suits out of the coins, but his pride and joy is his jumpsuit made out of no fewer than 3,568 of them. It took him 800 hours to make and it weighs 32 lb (15 kg). Just in case anyone has any doubt as to Steve's obsession, he also drives around in a van covered in 90,000 pennies.

The King and I
Paul MacLeod claims to be Elvis' number one fan—he even called his son Elvis Aaron Presley MacLeod. On show at Graceland Too, his house in Holly Springs, Mississippi, are Elvis' 1951 report card, a gold lamé suit supposedly worn by the King for a 1957 concert, and a casket that plays "Return to Sender," in which Paul plans to be buried.

U.S.A.
Connecticut

It is illegal for any beautician to hum, whistle, or sing while working on a customer.

ALL SHOOK UP

- Elvis had an eighth-degree black belt in karate

- Elvis was presented with a special award for helping to sell more popcorn in movie theatres from 1956 to 1957

- Elvis was obsessed with brushing his teeth

- Elvis would wear a football helmet while watching his favorite sport on TV

- 3,166 floral arrangements were delivered to Graceland on the two days following Elvis's death in 1977

- In the Islamic state of Mogadishu, in Somalia, it is illegal to impersonate Elvis without a beard

Sweet on Pez
"They're fun, they're cute, they're small," says Gary Doss, creator of the Burlingame Museum of Pez Memorabilia in California. He's describing Pez candy dispensers —and Gary should certainly know. For, since starting his collection in 1988, he has amassed hundreds of different dispensers, including ones with character heads of Mary Poppins, Mickey Mouse, Batman, and Santa Claus.

Overexposed
Photographer Spencer Tunick is driven by the urge to photograph masses of nude bodies in public places. He favors famous locations, such as New York City's Grand Central Station. Since 1992, he has staged his work on every continent, using up to 7,000 volunteers at once.

Breaking the Mold
Percy Westmore, known as "Perc," amassed a collection of Hollywood personality head molds.

Legal Eagle
In March 2004, 73-year-old Haskell Wexler, of Phoenix, Arizona, was in his 12th year of contesting three $31 (£16) parking tickets. The dispute has so far cost him 12 failed lawsuits and almost daily phone calls ($5,000).

The Bottom Line
Over the past 30 years, Barney Smith has painted more than 600 toilet seats, which are on display in his garage in Alamo Heights, Texas.

Chain Gang
Stan Willis's life changed forever the moment he bought a small padlock at a flea market in the late 1960s. He began collecting padlocks seriously, before abandoning them in favor of handcuffs. Now Stan, from Cincinnati, Ohio, has more than 900 pairs of handcuffs. Not content with that, he also collects leg irons, restraint chains, fire and police department badges, fire lanterns, and fire helmets.

That Really Sucks
California-based production artist Charlie Lester has been obsessed with vacuum cleaners since early childhood. He has acquired about 140 vintage vacuums (dating from 1905 to 1960) in the past four decades, and is an active member of the Vacuum Cleaner Collectors Club.

Well Done
Nearly 20 years ago, Deborah Henson-Conant got distracted and left a pot of cider on the stove for too long, and was fascinated by the result. Inspired, she decided to create the Burnt Food Museum to showcase all of her culinary disasters. Unfortunately, the museum, which is located in Arlington, Massachusetts, had to be temporarily closed in 2004—due to fire damage.

Do You Take this Superman?
Marcella Encinas was convinced that her husband-to-be, actor Scott Cranford, was her real-life Superman. Therefore, when the couple were looking for a suitable wedding venue in June 2001, they chose Metropolis, Illinois, the self-styled home of Superman, and arranged for Scott to attend the ceremony dressed in full Superman costume. Wonder Woman was the matron of honor, and Robin, Batman's sidekick, was the best man. Among the guests was a dog wearing a cape!

The Man in Green
"Berney" of Jacksonville, Florida, loved the color green so much that he dressed from head to toe in green, lived in a green house, had green furniture, and owned a restaurant decorated entirely in green.

DINE WITH "THE MAN IN GREEN" TRADE NAME REG. FROM RIPLEY'S "BELIEVE IT OR NOT"

SOUTH'S MOST TALKED OF PLACE TO DINE

Berney's RESTAURANT BAR AND MIRROR COCKTAIL LOUNGE JACKSONVILLE FLORIDA

A COLORFUL LIFE

JUST AS ACTOR Yul Brynner only wore black for 45 years, so Jean Rath of Santa Maria, California, is obsessed with purple.

She has lilac hair, wears purple clothes, drives only purple cars (with "I Love Purple" bumper stickers), and her business cards and checks name her as "The Purple Lady." She lives in a lavender house, with a lavender mailbox and fence. Of course everything inside is purple too—her violet toilet paper has to be ordered from Canada. Her late husband Bill also wore purple.

Everything in Jean Rath's house has to be purple—unable to buy a fridge or dishwasher in her favorite color, she simply painted them purple.

It's not difficult to see why British folk musician Cresby Brown is known as "Mr Red." He dresses from head to foot in bright scarlet and owns a wealth of red accessories.

Stringing Us Along
Vijayakanth of India is able to insert a nylon thread through his tear duct and pull it out through his mouth in just 60 seconds.

Carrying the Can
For years, John Milkovisch saved all his old beer cans. He eventually found a use for the can collection: slicing off the tops and bottoms, flattening the sides, and using the metal to cover the exterior of his house in Houston, Texas. He then linked the pull tabs and tops and bottoms of the cans to make curtains, wind chimes, windmills, and sculptures. He even made a beer-can canopy over his driveway and repaired his fence with cans. In 20 years of can construction, he has used more than 39,000 cans.

Shock Treatment
A holy man in northern India touches live electricity wires every day—for kicks. Sadhu Mangal Das, aka "Current Baba," touches a naked wire at least three times a day.

In the Can
Richard Sangster, from the Netherlands, began collecting soft-drinks cans in 1983 and now has more than 10,000, including a German series of Backstreet Boys Pepsi cans.

Book Him!
In 2001, police drove 120 mi (190 km) to LeRoy Anderson's home in Mapleton, Minnesota, brandishing an arrest warrant—because he had forgotten to return two overdue library books.

The Tin Man
This sculpture of a man, made from Coca-Cola tins was made by Teresa Roza and stands on display at the Ripley's museum in San Francisco.

Ripley's®
COKE CAN FIGURE
EXHIBIT NO: **15932**
CREATED FROM FLATTENED COKE TINS, THIS MALE FIGURE IS LIFE-SIZE

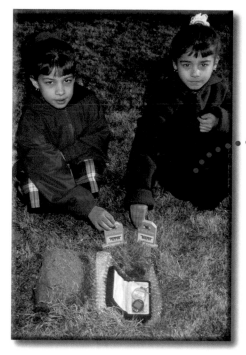

Beyond the Grave

Los Angeles is home to the Virtual Pet Cemetery for Tamagotchis, where bereaved children can go to pay their last respects to their dearly departed virtual friends.

Going by the Wayside

Over a period of 14 years, Fred Smith, a retired lumberjack from Phillips, Wisconsin, sculpted a cast of bizarre characters in concrete. More than 200 of his figures—including cowboys, miners, soldiers, and various animals—still stand by the wayside, and many of them are decorated with beer bottles from Smith's own tavern.

Concrete Proof

Benedictine monk Joseph Zoettel dedicated his life to constructing models of religious landmarks. He spent 50 years making miniature versions of buildings such as the Colosseum and the Vatican. Brother Joseph died in 1961, but 125 of his concrete reproductions are still exhibited at the Ave Maria Grotto at Cullman, Alabama.

Vintage Fashion

German fashion designer Josefine Edle von Krepl has spent her life collecting old clothes. She has hoarded more than 3,000 garbage can bags full of used garments, many dating back to the 1920s, because she could never bear to throw anything away.

Bus Fair

Geoff Price of Walsall, England, has spent the past 44 years collecting toy buses. He has nearly 8,000 models from around the world, and his hobby takes up so much space that he and his wife have been forced to move to a bigger house three times.

Island of the Dolls

For 50 years, Julian Santana scoured the garbage dumps of Mexico City. He was looking for discarded dolls, which he then hung from trees on an island in the city's Teshuilo Lake, where he lived alone. He collected thousands, helped by locals who would take boats to the island and exchange old dolls for the vegetables he grew.

Read All About It

Artist Ronald Max Vollmer produced a unique maze constructed from more than 50,000 old books! Vollmer spent a large part of his life as a scientist but, inspired by his painter father, he always dreamed of becoming an artist. Since the 1990s, he has developed his own style of installation art. One such piece was a trail of lit lamps being carried through his family home. More recently, he embarked on the book maze. Visitors to the maze could wind their way through passages constructed from books stacked high upon one another. Not only could visitors view the piece, but they could also leave their own mark on the installation, by adding their own books if they wished.

Vollmer adds the finishing touches to the 50,000-strong book maze!

A Perfect Match
Prateep Tankanchanrverukul, from Thailand, has a collection of more than 100,000 matchboxes, including some rare ones. He has even made a jacket out of some of the matchboxes in his collection and claims to wear it wherever he goes.

Magnetic Personality
Over the past 30 years, Louise J. Greenfarb of Las Vegas, Nevada, has collected more than 29,000 fridge magnets, including some featuring portraits of sports heroes, cartoon characters, and presidents. Her ambition is to be buried in her fridge, surrounded by a thousand of her favorite magnets.

In at the Deep End
A Chinese pensioner called Yan performs a daily exercise of walking backward around Bayi Lake because he believes it is good for his health. Unfortunately, in April 2003 he was so busy counting his steps that he lost his bearings, fell in, and had to be rescued by fellow walkers.

Dear Diary...
For no less than four hours a day, every day since 1972, Robert Shields of Dayton, Washington, has typed out a record of absolutely everything that has happened to him. His diary, which at 38 million words is thought to be the world's longest, is stored in more than 80 cardboard boxes. An example of his attention to detail is: "July 25, 1993, 7 a.m.: I cleaned out the tub and scraped my feet with my fingernails to remove layers of dead skin." He has also kept every check that he has written over the past 60 years.

Every Night at the Movies
Derek Atkins of York, England, has visited Odeon cinemas eight times a week since 1988. But he doesn't go to watch the movies—he goes to study the décor. Derek, who used to work for Odeon as an usher and projectionist, admits he is obsessed with the Odeon chain. "If I can't see a film at the Odeon, I won't go and see it," he says.

Buzz Off
In 1998, Californian Mark Biancaniello was covered in an estimated 350,000 bees, weighing a total of 87.5 lb (40 kg).

Gone to Pot
The Portable Border installation consisted of 100 plant pots in a line, which stretched as far as 40 ft (12 m). That wasn't all there was to this piece of art, because the flowery line moved approximately 2.5 mi (4 km) through the streets of London, England, during April 2004! British artist Phil Coy simply took the plant at the back of the line and moved it to the front, then took the next plant at the back and moved that to the front, and so on until he eventually reached his destination!

Phil Coy had exhibited his flower art in Germany and Finland, before moving it to the streets of London, England.

Dotty!

KAREN FERRIER IS dotty about spots!

It all started 12 years ago with her Dalmatian dog, Ditto, but now she has a spotted car, spotted clothes, spotted hats, spotted shoes, and a spotted room. She also used to have a spotted motorbike, which she rode in a spotted helmet and spotted leathers. Her remaining ambition is to paint the outside of her house in Southampton, England... with spots, of course.

Spot the Dog

Esther the Dalmatian ran away for three days in October 2003—high-tailing it down a highway, swimming across San Francisco Bay, and running down Runway 28 at San Francisco International Airport.

The Cat's Whiskers

"Stalking Cat," also known as Dennis Avner, a Californian computer repair man, is gradually transforming himself into a feline through painful plastic surgery. "Cat," as he is commonly known, developed his obsession with all things feline at the age of 23, when he had his first tattoo—of tiger stripes. Now 44, "Cat" is covered in striped tattoos. He has even gone so far as to have plastic surgery to give him a cleft lip, synthetic whisker implants, and elongated ears.

Serial Groom

Udaynath Dakshiniray, 80, from Orali, India, has been married no fewer than 90 times. Nobly, he has always chosen poor brides so that he could spread a little of his own wealth. He hopes to clock up a century of wives before he dies.

Splitting Hairs

Leila Cohoon collects hair, but not just any old hair: it must be human hair dating from before 1900. Hair art has been her passion for more than 40 years. Leila's Hair Museum in Independence, Missouri, features jewelry, wreaths, and pictures. Her favorite item is a 19th-century floral tapestry made from the hair of 156 members of one family.

Hair Today...

In the Victorian era, wreaths were made from the hair of a dead person and their relatives. These were placed on the coffin during funeral services and later hung in the family home.

Walmart Worship

Derek's Big Website of Walmart Purchase Receipts is run by Derek Dahlsad of Dilworth, Minnesota. He has posted every Walmart receipt he's received since 1996 and asks visitors to comment on purchases from power tools to baby wipes.

Hair Shirt

St. Louis barber Bill Black has made several items of clothing such as dresses, socks, hats, mittens, and even a bikini—from nothing other than human hair!

Ripley's®
HAIR WREATH
EXHIBIT NO: 4897
ORIGINATES FROM THE 1880s AND WAS
PURCHASED BY RIPLEYS IN 1995

Ripley's®
HUMAN VEST HAIR
EXHIBIT NO: 13817
CREATED BY BARBER, BILL BLACK,
MADE ENTIRELY FROM HAIR

Trunk Call

Ever since receiving his first ornamental elephant as a gift from his sister-in-law on his wedding day in 1967, Ed Gotwalt has had a thing about pachyderms. His collection soon grew and his wife suggested he open a museum. Today, Mr. Ed's Elephant Museum in Orrtanna, Pennsylvania, is home to more than 6,000 elephants made from just about every known substance. In his spare time, Ed tours the country selling elephants' favorite food—peanuts!

The Long Way Home

In 2002, a Japanese canoeist finished a 5,965-mi (9,600-km) journey around the country's coast... 23 years after he started! Reiji Yoshioka began his adventure in 1979 from near his home in Kanagawa, and always fitted it in with his work as a printer. He was 64 when he completed the final leg of his trip around the northern island of Hokkaido.

Word Perfect

An Indian man has memorized the entire *Oxford Advanced Learners' Dictionary*. It took Mahaveer Jain just ten months to remember each of the 80,000 individual entries. He can also recall their exact sequence and the page on which they appear.

Beatlemania

Beatle-mad Argentinean Rodolfo Vazquez keeps more than 5,600 items of Fab Four memorabilia in his loft. Among his most treasured possessions are some bricks from the Cavern Club in Liverpool, England, where the Beatles first played.

Salad Days

Radish fanatics can celebrate their devotion to this underrated vegetable every December 23 at the Night of the Radishes exhibition in Oaxaca, Mexico. Huge radishes are carved into highly detailed figures and displayed in intricate scenes that reflect the local culture.

Venerable Beads

Over a period of 13 months, working eight hours a day, Faris Hassan, of Amman, Jordan, used more than 175,000 beads to make a 23-ft (7-m) long rosary.

a Man of bEaNS

Captain Beany lives his life as a baked bean. The tomato sauce-soaked food gets his pulse racing so much that he regularly plunges into a bathtub full of them.

BARRY KIRK, AKA CAPTAIN BEANY, is bean mad! In fact he loves baked beans so much that he has officially changed his name to Captain Beany.

He drives a baked bean illustrated car, drinks baked bean cocktails, paints himself orange, and dons a baked bean costume! He wears an orange jumpsuit and cape and even paints his bald head orange. When he needed a passport to match his new identity, he produced a completely orange photo of himself. Naturally, he eats baked beans every day.

Bean Feats

In June 2004, Hollywood celebrated the 30th anniversary of the blockbuster movie *Blazing Saddles*, by producing a special edition DVD promotion. The event was happily celebrated at the Saddle Ranch Chop House in the heart of Hollywood and was marked with a human "bean dip" contest. Movie fans took turns to dive in and search through the beans for a *Blazing Saddles* DVD.

A stalwart Blazing Saddles *fan scrambles in a vat of baked beans for the DVD.*

Claiming to hail from Planet Beanus, on Earth Captain Beany uses a mode of transport that is much more suitable for human "beans."

His motto is "to baldly go where no man has bean before" and to that end he founded the New Millennium Bean Party, polling 122 votes in the 2001 general election.

The 50-year-old Captain, who recently paid $750 to insure himself against alien abduction, plans to turn his apartment in Port Talbot, South Wales, into a bean museum. However, there is a downside to being Captain Beany. "I've been out of work since 1992," says Kirk, "because I've changed my name and dress up as Captain Beany. . . a job for a superhero is very hard to come by." Just don't let anyone call him a "has-bean!"

Bean Bathtub
Danny Cooper, a computer student from Kings Lynn, England, raised money for charity by immersing himself for two hours in a bathtub full of cold baked beans.

MGH 726L

Veg Out

Who said vegetables are boring? This selection of odd-shaped veg includes "aero-potato," grown by J.J. Brophy, Oregon.

A Light Lunch

An Indian man has been eating pieces of glass and empty liquor bottles for the past 20 years. P. Arthanari Swamy found he could digest glass when he crushed some in his drink during a failed suicide attempt. Now his mother often serves him glass bulbs and bottles with his dinner. The only glass items he can't eat are soda bottles, which are too thick. When he wants a change, he eats lead bullets!

Hold the Mayo!

Weighing 6,991 lb (3,178 kg), this giant sandwich was made by workers in Mexico City in 2004.

Bearing Fruit
Camilla Bowitz from Worcester, England, had a special fruit tree growing in her back garden—it bore both apples and plums!

Don't Forget to Floss
Diane DeCair of Toledo, Ohio, likes to inhale strands of spaghetti up her nose. In fact, by carefully sniffing and coughing, she can simultaneously pull one end of the pasta from her nose and the other from her mouth, in a flossing motion. "It's kind of disgusting to watch," she admits.

The Spitting Image
The International Cherry Pit Spitting Championship at Eau Claire, Michigan, has turned into a real family affair. Rick Krause has won the title 12 times, and in 2004 his son Brian completed a hat-trick of wins with a spit of 88 ft 2 in (26.8 m), just 5 ft (1.5 m) short of his 2003 record. Rick actually married his wife Marlene at the contest. Naturally, she's an ace spitter too.

Forever Blowing Bubbles
Susan Montgomery Williams of Fresno, California, has been America's "Bubble Queen" since 1979. After discovering that the existing record for blowing bubblegum was a modest 17 in (43 cm) bubble, Susan told the Bubble Yum Company that she could blow a 20 in (50 cm) bubble with just three pieces of gum. They didn't believe her, until she arrived blowing a bubble the size of a basketball with one breath. She won an unlimited supply of bubblegum as long as she held the record. Over 25 years later, she still holds it with a blow of 23 in (58 cm).

U.S.A. Maine
In Portland, shoelaces must be tied while walking down the street.

Make Yourself at Home
A burglar broke into a dozen Seattle homes in August 2004 to raid... the fridges. Ignoring the jewelry, in one home he ate six shrimp kebabs, 12 mini corndogs, half a pack of cooked meat, 12 balls of frozen cookie dough, handfuls of candies, a box of Creamsicles, two fruit drinks, and a glass of milk. In another break-in he thawed and fried frozen steaks and ate them while watching TV—until he was disturbed by the homeowners!

Dip In

While 20 per cent of the U.S.A.'s population eat 48 per cent of the avocados consumed each year, Super Bowl Sunday is the biggest day of the year for avocado consumption. Industry executives estimate that more than 43 million lb (19.5 million kg) are eaten during the football game, most of it in the form of guacamole dip.

Dog Eat Dog

At age ten, "Krazy" Kevin Lipsitz from Staten Island, New York, could eat ten ears of corn in a sitting. Now a speed-eating champ, he once ate 2 lb (1 kg) of sour pickles in five minutes, and his wife, Lorain, also competes as "Loraineasaurus Rex." Kevin trains with his two dogs. "I cook up a family pack of 40 hot dogs and we race. But we don't eat out of the same bowl."

Impeccable Taste

Wilma Beth Shulke of Mission, Texas, created her own easter outfit made from sliced cross-sections of corn cobs, trimmed with orange peel.

A Brush with Death

Surgeons in India removed a toothbrush from a man's stomach a week after he accidentally swallowed it. Anil Kumar apparently swallowed the toothbrush while brushing his teeth in front of the TV, but only went to the hospital when the pain became unbearable.

Ripley's®
LINT ART
EXHIBIT NO: 13989
SUSHI AND CANDY MADE BY SLATER BARRON
ENTIRELY OUT OF LINT

Hair-brained Scheme

Gary Arnold has a unique method of charging customers who visit his restaurant in Lodi, California—he charges them according to the amount of hair on their head. The hairiest pay most, and bald people eat for free!

Sweet as Candy

Slater Barron's friends and neighbors collect lint for her, which she stores in boxes in her studio/garage. She then sorts the lint according to color before creating the art.

DRESSING for DINNER

FASHION DESIGNER Alessandro Consiglio cooked up a storm on the runways of Rome, Italy, in 2002.

Using vacuum-packed meat (including salami, ham, and pastrami) instead of conventional fabrics, the exotic fashion designer created a feast for more than just the eyes as models showed off the meaty masterpieces to applauding onlookers.

Consiglio's dresses are made from many different types of salami and ham.

Bread Winner

As part of his Pain Couture exhibition in Paris, fashion designer Jean Paul Gaultier celebrated the artistry of French bakers by creating dresses, boots, bags, and even thongs, from dough.

Speak for Yourself

Known as "Bread Head," Japanese artist Tatsumi Orimoto spent June 1996 strolling through London with baguettes tied to his head. Earlier, he had spent two years in Germany with a 9-ft (3-m) chimney in his backpack and five years with a cardboard box on his foot. He passed another year dragging an iron bath round New York's Greenwich Village. "It's my way of communicating," he says.

Gross Interest

Whereas most people like to pop chocolate into their mouth, John LaMedica prefers live cockroaches. The man known as "Jungle John" stuffed a record nine poisonous Madagascan cockroaches into his mouth at the same time during a *Ripley's Believe It Or Not!* TV show in 2003. John, from Newark, Delaware, admits his act is "really gross." He adds: "They hiss and have spikes on their legs that cut the inside of my mouth, and sometimes they defecate in your mouth, but you can't do much about it. It leaves a bitter taste."

Chew it Over

Seattle's unlikeliest tourist attraction is the Gum Wall in Pike Place Market. The entire wall is covered in thousands of pieces of chewing-gum in all colors from the mouths of people from all over the world.

Breaking Bread

A church in Buffalo, New York, has decided that visitors should be able to grab lunch while worshiping. The True Bethel Baptist Church is the first in the U.S.A. to open its own Subway restaurant.

Radiator Grill

Dave Curtis of Suffolk, England, converted his Skoda car into a wheely unusual barbeque!

Chickening Out

Kay Martin freaked out when the chicken she was cooking began to squawk. Steam had built up in the bird and was escaping through its vocal cords. Put off, Martin threw it out and hasn't cooked chicken since.

Champion Biscuit

The world's biggest ham biscuit was prepared at Smithfield, Virginia, in 2002. Made from 500 lb (230 kg) of ham, it measured a staggering 8 ft wide and 14 in (36 cm) tall.

Don't Bug Me

Students at the Iowa State University Entomology Club don't just study six-legged bugs, they also eat them! Particular favorite accompaniments are a cajun sauce, covered in chocolate... or just dipped in Jell-O.

Ice-breakers

In a bid to boost sales, Japanese confectioners introduced an exciting new range of ice-creams in 2002. Customers could cool down with such exotic flavors as octopus, horseradish, shark's fin, garlic, potato and lettuce, whale, and cactus, not to mention basashi vanilla, which contained chunks of raw horse-flesh! Meanwhile, a British restaurateur has started serving bacon-and-egg ice-cream.

Some of the exotic ice-cream flavors the Japanese invented during the scorching summer of 2002.

BY GUM!

- Between 1992 and 2004, chewing-gum was banned in Singapore as it messed up streets and trains. Gum dealers face jail if they break the rules
- In 2003, students at a school in Washington persuaded teachers to let them chew gum in class because scientific tests showed that it increased the blood flow to brain cells
- Furious at seeing the Russian soccer team chewing gum rather than singing the national anthem at Euro 2004, President Putin ordered all gum in Russia to be confiscated

Benjie Moss, a student at Staffordshire University in England, created this life-sized sculpture of the long-extinct Dodo bird after he gave up smoking and started chewing gum to alleviate his cravings. Rather than discarding the gum, he put it to good use making this sculpture!

Long-distance Call

When you visit a McDonald's drive-thru, no matter where you are, it's quite possible that your order is routed through a call center in Colorado Springs, Colorado. Within 30 seconds, the order you shout into the microphone is typed into a computer in Colorado and then routed back to that same McDonald's kitchen. The system apparently creates fewer errors.

Emergency Rations

A U.S. Army laboratory has developed a dried meal that can be hydrated with dirty water or, if absolutely necessary, a soldier's own urine. This is possible because a special membrane allows only water molecules to pass through and filters out more than 99 per cent of bacteria and most chemicals.

Gum Blondes

Artist Jason Kronewald, from Toronto, Ontario, creates portraits of celebrities that appear to be made out of clay but are actually sculpted from chewing-gum. He doesn't like to chew gum himself, but instead persuades his friends to soften it up for his use. His *Gum Blondes* series includes singer Britney Spears and actress Pamela Anderson.

Great Britney

Britney Spears' fans clearly don't think the pop star's chewed gum is toxic—because they bought some of it on eBay. On the Internet site in September 2004, there were more than two dozen auctions of chewing-gum, which people claimed had been spat out by Britney. Most pieces sold for around $50 (£25), although fake bidding almost pushed the price as high as $14,000 (£7,400)!

Having a Ball

Eric "Badlands" Booker, a 34-year-old 395-lb (180-kg) heavyweight has for the second year in a row, become the Matzo Ball Contest champ. In 2003, Booker earned a world record by wolfing down 21 of the baseball-size dumplings, which are made from meal, eggs, and chicken broth. In 2004, the subway operator gobbled up just 20 of the 5-oz (140-g) balls in the allotted 5 minutes and 25 seconds, but still won. He prepared by eating 10 lb (4.5 kg) of cabbage three nights before the contest.

Nutty Protester

To demonstrate his support for English culture and food, performance artist Mark McGowan decided to turn himself into a full English breakfast. For 12 days in November 2003, McGowan sat in a London shop window in a bath of baked beans, with two chips up his nose and 48 sausages wrapped around his head. Earlier in the year, he had protested against student debt by using his nose to roll a peanut along 7 mi (11 km) of London roads to the Prime Minister's door at 10 Downing Street.

A Colossal Appetite

In 1999, pizza-maker Jeff Parker from Brooks in Alberta, Canada, came up with the world's biggest commercially available pizza. Called the "Colossal," it measures 3 ft (90 cm) wide and 4 ft (1.2 m) long, and serves 108 people.

My Head's Spinning

Now you can wash your dirty laundry in public and drink a cocktail at the same time! The Laundry Bar in Miami, Florida, is an ordinary launderette but it also has a fully stocked and licensed bar.

U.S.A.
Georgia

No one may carry an ice-cream cone in their back pocket on a Sunday.

The Tipping Point

A 2003 survey of Domino's Pizza managers in the Washington D.C. area found that the day Saddam Hussein was captured, December 13, 2003, was the biggest day of the year for tips, and orders for meat-topped pies were the highest in two years.

To Diet For

No willpower? Then "DDS," a new dental appliance, might help. The dental plate fits on the roof of the mouth and prevents people from shoveling in large quantities of food. One study has shown the $400 (£200) device helped people to lose more than 1 lb (0.5 kg) a week.

Wakey Wakey

A Minnesota dairy has begun producing milk that is spiked with caffeine. Called "Hyper Cow," the frothy breakfast staple contains as much caffeine and sugar as a can of soda.

Bean Feast

Tracy Ostmann loves to make jellybean art. She was once commissioned to create a jellybean painting of a great white shark for a Chicago aquarium. More recently, she produced a 15-color portrait of Martin Luther King Jr. While Ostmann loves her medium, she says she has to refrain from eating too many of the beans while working, just in case she makes herself sick.

Grow Your Own

Giles Peare, a farmer from West Sussex, in England, eats grubs, worms, and insects that he finds on his farm.

No LicKiNG!

THE WORLD'S FIRST—and only—hotel made entirely of salt has a "no licking" policy.

Built on the world's largest salt bed, the Uyuni Salt Hotel is located west of Colchani, deep in the salt plains of Bolivia, South America. Passing the salt will never be a problem, as the salt will always be on the table—in fact, like everything else, the table is made of salt.

Vinegar Joes

Vinegar-lovers gather in South Dakota, for the annual Vinegar Festival. Top prize goes to the Mother of All Vinegars contest winner. There's also a tasting at the vinegar museum—sugar cubes are then supplied to freshen contestants' mouths.

The Uyuni Salt Hotel is the only hotel in the world that is made entirely from salt.

Even the hotel beds are made from salt crystals.

Ripley's — Believe It or Not!®

On Ice

An 81-year-old Indian woman has eaten huge chunks of ice every day for the last 17 years to relieve stomach ache. Shanti Devi eats up to 22 lb (10 kg) a day in the summer, and says she can't sleep without her daily ice intake, most of it from neighbors' refrigerators.

Pizza the Action

In August 1998, a company called Little Caesar's took an order from jeans manufacturer the VF Corporation of Greensboro, North Carolina, for 13,386 pizzas—to feed 40,160 employees at 180 locations in the U.S.A.

Fungi Fun

Weighing over 21 lb (9.5 kg), this edible giant puffball fungus was discovered by A.B. Tyler near his home in New York.

BEAN SCENE

- The navy bean got its name because it was an essential part of the US Navy's diet in the 19th century
- The navy bean is the official vegetable of Massachusetts
- A restaurant dedicated solely to the culinary delights of baked navy beans opened in Melbourne, Australia, in 2004
- Native Americans flavored their baked navy beans with maple syrup
- West Bromwich, England, has been dubbed The Windy City after a survey found its inhabitants to be the UK's biggest fans of baked beans

Sugar Sugar

Mary Horton is addicted to sugar—she eats an average of 2 lb (1 kg) of it every day!

A Big Fish

By swallowing 350 live minnows in under an hour, Shane Williams of Wonder Lake, Chicago, smashed the existing record of 280 set in 1998.

Naked Lunch?

At Germany's Bellview Restaurant the menus are painted on the bare skin of the waiters and waitresses.

Super Cucumber

Willian H. Rainey of Fort Worth, Texas grew a cucumber to an amazing 4 ft 11 in (1.3 m)!

80

Bean Cuisine

After taking part in a bean cook-off, contestants in the annual Bean Fest at Mountain View, Arkansas, then compete in an "outhouse race."

Stab in the Pack

A Michigan housewife was rushed to the hospital after accidentally stabbing herself with a shard of pasta. It entered her finger with such force that doctors had to remove part of her fingernail.

Shell Shock

Norwegian Rune Naeri swallowed 187 oysters in three minutes—more than one per second—at the 2003 Hillsborough Oyster Festival in Northern Ireland. His total almost doubled the previous world record.

Biting the Bullet

Eating a hot dog in May 2004, Californian Olivia Chanes bit on something hard. When she began complaining of a metallic taste in her mouth, doctors discovered that she had swallowed a 0.4 in (9 mm) bullet!

The Worms Turn

In November 2003, C. Manoharan swallowed 200 live earthworms in just 20 seconds on a beach in the Indian port of Chennai. Each worm was 4 in (10 cm) long, and it took him a year to prepare for the feat.

Ice and a Slice?

This giant lemon grew in a hot house in Chippenham, England. Compared to this ordinary-sized lemon, it sure is a whopper!

Sourpusses!

A St. Louis health commissioner has apologized to Mim Murray, 10, and Marisa Miller-Stockie, 12, after a city inspector shut down their lemonade stand for operating without a business license. The girls were just trying to raise money to buy laptop computers. The city later admitted that it was overzealous in its attempt to enforce its food and vendor permit rules.

COFFEE BREAK

- In 17th-century Turkey, anyone who was caught drinking coffee was executed

- According to Harvard research, regular coffee-drinkers have less chance of having asthma

- The Japanese bath in ground coffee to improve their skin

Spam Cram

First held in 1978, Spamarama attracts thousands of Spamophiles to Austin, Texas, to an annual celebration of the famous tinned meat. Events include a Spam toss, a Spam-calling contest, and a Spam-eating competition, known as the "Spam Cram."

Eggstra Large

Take more than 5,000 eggs, add 50 lb (23 kg) of onions, 75 green bell peppers, 52 lb (24 kg) of butter, over 6 gal (23 l) of milk, 4 gal (15 l) of green onion tops, 2 gal (8 l) of parsley, some crawfish tails, and Tabasco pepper sauce to taste, and what have you got?... the Giant Omelette of Abbeville, Louisiana, which keeps on getting bigger each year. The Giant Omelette Celebration began in 1984 with 5,000 eggs, and one egg has been added every year since.

Toe Sandwich

A 35-year-old Austrian man, hungry for a snack, hacked off the toes on his left foot, fried them, and ate them between two slices of bread—because he could find nothing else to eat! When ambulance staff arrived, the man offered a toe, saying it tasted like chicken!

U.S.A. Georgia

In Gainesville, chicken may only legally be eaten using ones fingers instead of cutlery.

Burns' Night Blast-off

In 2002, Canadian businessman Gordon Sinclair announced that, as part of the Robert Burns' Night celebrations, he had patented a Haggis Launcher in order to propel a 1 lb (454 g) haggis across Calgary's huge Bow River!

A Sting in the Tale

Dorset, England, is home to the World Stinging Nettle Eating Championships, in which competitors eat their way through the stinging, itching plant. Ouch!

Eat Your Art Out
Forget paints—this carpet is being painted with food including cream and custard!

Eating Around the World
While he was rating the quality of diners around the world, Chicago food critic Fred E. Magel visited 46,000 restaurants in 60 countries over a period of 50 years.

There's the Grub
A Thai firefighter named Paisit Chanta thinks the key to a healthy life is to eat a live worm every single day. He has done so for 30 years and says that he had suffered nothing worse than mild flu.

Let Them Eat Cake
Drew Cerza, of Buffalo, New York, came up with a way to help others unload their unwanted holiday fruitcakes without tossing them in the trash. He asked for 100,000 cakes to be sent to him so that he could forward them to a food bank for the needy. His only stipulation was that the fruitcake be no more than two years old.

Double Trouble
An Israeli woman swallowed a fork in 2003 while trying to retrieve a cockroach from her throat. The insect jumped into her mouth while she was brushing her teeth, but when she tried to scoop it out with a fork, she swallowed that too.

It's No Turkey
Seattle soft drinks firm Jones Soda Co. introduced a turkey-and-gravy flavored fizzy drink for Christmas 2003. The novelty line proved to be so successful that it very quickly sold out, leaving thirsty customers clamoring for more.

When the Chips are Down
Nicknamed a "compulsive swallower," a man in the 1930s was reported to have swallowed several poker chips. This X-ray shows the chips inside the man's stomach.

Mouse Trap
In the 1940s, Dagmar Rothman performed a stunt at Ripley's New York City Odditorium in which he swallowed lemons and a mouse—and then regurgitated them.

UMmm... NiCe!?!

Matthew gets stuck on to a chewy treat.

MATTHEW BIANCANIELLO proved that he can eat anything during a 2002 *Ripley's* TV show.

Matthew's feat is not for the weak-stomached to watch! His eat-anything menu includes such treats as animal eyeballs, cow dung, a cow's and bull's muscles, leeches, maggots, and fish intestines.

Matthew considers the many delicacies he intends to devour during his act.

Grubs, maggots, and worms... delicious!

I believe that's an eyeball he's eating!

Matthew takes a pause before consuming yet another sumptuous snack!

Delivering the Goods

In 1998, Manhattan restaurant-owner Eddie Fishbaum was asked to deliver a plain pizza to TV host Eiji Bando in Tokyo, a distance of 6,753 mi (10,130 km). The pizza cost $7,000 (£3,600) including Eddie's airfare.

Brain Box

Etta's Lunch Box Café in Logan, Ohio, is decorated with owner Ladora Ouesley's collection of more than 400 lunchboxes. If customers point out the type of box they used to carry to school, Ladora can correctly identify the year they began their education.

Bite Size

Philadelphia confectioner Glenn Mueller Jr. has introduced a line of chocolate body parts. Enjoy the smooth texture of chocolate hearts, brains, lungs, and even dentures. If you can't resist one naughty bite, try the Mike Tyson special—a chocolate ear with a chunk missing!

Human Piggy Bank

When treated for stomach pains, a 62-year-old Frenchman was found to have swallowed 350 coins (francs and euros), plus assorted necklaces and needles. They weighed 12 lb (5 kg), as much as a bowling ball. The man, who died shortly afterwards, had been swallowing coins for ten years despite his family's attempts to wean him off them.

Fowl Play

A two-hour jail riot which resulted in an estimated $10,000 (£5,000) worth of damage was sparked by the poor quality of a chicken dinner! Inmates at Autry State Prison in Pelham, Georgia, smashed lights, destroyed sprinkler heads, broke windows, and set fire to mattresses in December 2001 after one of the prisoners complained that his chicken was not thoroughly cooked.

Knit Wit

Eileen Mulrooney made a special kind of cake for her daughter's wedding. It looked yummy, but eating it wouldn't have been a pleasant experience—the whole cake was made from knitted wool!

Lord of the Flies

A man named Farook has taken to eating a diet consisting solely of flies in protest at his council's garbage-collection service. The social worker says that garbage left in the streets of Tirunelveli, western India, is attracting swarms of the insects.

Piece of Cake

Training instructor Robert Jones cut his 50th birthday cake while doing a one-handed handstand. Other feats included doing a handstand with 200 lb (90 kg) of weights tied around his waist.

Hen-pecked

Jan Csovary from Prievidza, Slovakia, has eaten more than 11,000 chickens since being diagnosed as a diabetic in the early 1970s. He has chicken for breakfast, lunch, and tea, but has to cook it himself because his wife moaned that she was sick of the sight of chickens 20 years ago!

Spuds they Like

Every year, the town of Clark, South Dakota, stages a Potato Day in celebration of its favorite vegetable. The festivities include a Best Decorated Potato contest, potato sculptures and mashed-potato wrestling, in which the combatants fight each other in a ring full of mashed potato.

EXTRA PEPPERONI?

- There are approximately 61,300 pizzerias in the U.S.A. and over 9,000 in New York alone

- 94 per cent of the population of the U.S.A. eat pizza

- Americans eat about 100 acres (40 ha) of pizza each day, or about 350 slices per second

- Americans eat 251,770,000 lb (114,201,000 kg) of pepperoni, their favorite pizza topping, every year

- Red herring is the most popular pizza topping in Russia

- Unusual toppings created by pizza-makers include peanut butter and jelly, bacon and eggs, and mashed potatoes

Big Mouth

In 1998, American Johnny Reitz managed to cram three standard-sized hamburgers (including buns) into his mouth simultaneously without swallowing.

Beat That

Omelette fans had better head to Norma's, a restaurant in a hotel in Manhattan, New York, which sells a $1,000 (£515) "Zillion Dollar Frittata," surely the most expensive in the world. Made with six eggs, a whole lobster, and 10 oz (283 g) of caviar, the omelette started out as a simple Lobster Frittata. Chef Emile Castillo and the hotel's general manager Steven Pipes decided to experiment with different ingredients and soon discovered that adding caviar made it even more delicious. Its entry on the menu dares customers to experience it.

A "budget" version of the omelette is also available, which contains only 1 oz (28 g) of caviar and sells for $100 (£50).

The Breakfast Club

Since 1990, Springfield, Massachusetts, has been home to the world's largest pancake breakfast, at which an 1,800 ft (549 m) long table seats more than 75,000 people. The feast requires 2,700 lb (1,225 kg) of flour, 600 lb (272 kg) of eggs, 210 lb (95 kg) of butter, and 210 gal (795 l) of water, all topped with 450 gal (1,703 l) of maple syrup. The pancakes are served with 3,370 gal (12,757 l) of coffee and 1,150 gal (4,353 l) of orange juice.

On the Double

On October 11, 2004, Domino's Pizza offered a free medium double crust pizza to any New Yorker who could prove that they had the same first and last name. Via an online search, Domino's estimated that there were at least 30 locals who would be able to take advantage of the offer.

Winging it

Ed "Cookie" Jarvis is a man of taste. In fact, the speed-eater from Long Island, New York, holds records for consuming such diverse items as ice-cream, pasta, pork ribs, corned beef, and cabbage. He has also eaten 91 Chinese dumplings in eight minutes, 40 meatballs in four minutes, and 2 lb (907 g) of pickles in five minutes. He beat champion eater Sonya Thomas in a chicken-wing contest when he devoured 134 in just 12 minutes!

Choices, Choices

La Casa Gelato, in Vancouver, certainly knows ice-cream. The store offers customers nearly 500 flavors, although only 208 are available at any given time. Diversity in flavors apparently keeps customers coming back for more. The range includes such exotic tastes as curry, corn, durian, blue cheese, dandelion, garlic, vinegar, wasabi/green apple— and one that tastes like Guinness stout.

Big Cheese

Sculptors Jimm Scannell and Jim Victor created a life-sized replica of a race car using 3,500 lb (1,600 kg) of Cheddar cheese for the International Speedway in Richmond, Virginia.

Keen as Mustard

The first Saturday in August is Official Mustard Day in Mount Horeb, Wisconsin. Now in its 15th year, the celebration, held at the local mustard museum, features mustard tastings and a fiery cook-off.

HARD CHEESE

- Cheese was a form of currency in 16th-century Denmark

- A 1956 expedition to the South Pole found a tin of Edam cheese left behind by Captain Scott and his party in 1912. The cheese was still edible

- Blue Vinny cheese is so hard that a whole cheese was once used as a temporary wheel replacement on a train

- Cornish Yarg cheese is served coated in nettles

- In the 12th century, Blanche of Navarre tried to win the heart of the French king Philippe Auguste by sending him 200 cheeses every year

Carrot and Stick
Julie Tori from Southampton, England, has eaten between 4 lb (1.8 kg) and 5 lb (2.3 kg) of carrots every day for the past ten years. She did have one day off from munching her favorite vegetable—but was immediately seized by a panic attack.

Dynamic Duo
According to a recent survey by Mr. Clean and Magic Eraser, Americans simply can't resist spaghetti and meatballs. The dish took the title for "Favorite Food Duo," and macaroni and cheese, and milk and cereal were a close second and third.

Choc Tactics
This sculpture should have chocoholics watering at the mouth. Tokyo chef Daisuke Nogami took one month and used 550 lb (250 kg) of white chocolate to create an 80-in (206-cm) tall replica of the Venus de Milo statue. It was displayed at the Food Art Museum in Tokyo in 2003.

Pie in the Sky
According to Domino's Pizza, the five biggest days for pizza delivery in the U.S.A. are Super Bowl Sunday, Thanksgiving Eve, New Year's Day, New Year's Eve, and Halloween. Every week, Domino's drivers rack up 9 million mi (13.5 million km), which is further than 37 trips to the Moon and back.

Hard Graft
Paramedics in Stuart, Florida, worked up a sweat when trying to remove a 480-lb (218-kg) woman from her home. They knew the doorways would be tricky, but quickly discovered a much more pressing problem. The woman, who had not moved from her couch for several years, had to be carried out on it because the fabric had grafted on to her skin. Doctors surgically separated the woman from the couch, but she died in the hospital after breathing complications.

Yellow Peril
Californian Ken Bannister, known as "Banana Man," has amassed more than 17,000 banana-related objects since he founded the International Banana Club in 1972. He has a banana-shaped putter and yellow golf balls; books on bananas; a banana-shaped couch; banana-related art, clothing, food, and toiletries; plus banana-shaped telephones, lamps, clocks, watches, soft toys, crockery, and cutlery!

In the Soup
In Erie, Pennsylvania, Democrats at the Polish Falcons Club eat duck blood soup every election day!

Say Cheese!

Offbeat Canadian sculptor Cosimo Cavallaro doesn't work with ordinary art materials—he uses cheese! He has dressed a model from head to toe in cheese, sprayed jackets in cheese, and decorated a New York hotel room with dripping formaggio. In 2001, he even painted an entire house in Wyoming with 10,000 lb (4,500 kg) of sprayed-on mozzarella. Then, in 2004, to prove that he could work with other materials, he covered a bed at a Manhattan hotel with slices of a 308-lb (140-kg) processed ham.

It's Electrifying

It was an illuminating experience for Russian Alvarez Kanichka when he swallowed live lightbulbs—and then retrieved them by pulling on the electrical cord, still attached!

Seedy Art

New York artist Hugh McMahon loves to create art with watermelons. Weighing up to 50 lb (23 kg), most pieces take him two hours to complete.

Eat My Shorts

Stopped by cops, an 18-year-old driver from Stettler, Alberta, tried to eat his own underwear in the hope that the cotton fabric would absorb the alcohol before he took a breathalyzer test. Maybe it worked, because his test level was below the legal limit and he was acquitted.

Whistle While You Work

In 1934, Paul Williams of Nashville, Tennessee, placed four golf balls in his mouth and managed to whistle at the same time!

Melt Down

Originating at a campsite in Dorset, England, in 1997, cheese racing, as it's known, involves slices of processed cheese—still in their plastic wrapping—being thrown on to a hot barbeque by contestants. The cheese wrapper doesn't melt, and the first cheese slice to inflate, wins the cheese race!

Slippery Starter

Tequila-flavored lollipops contain caterpillars or scorpions.

BORED WITH BEANS on toast? Then Edible, a new restaurant in London, England, is the place to eat!

Created by Todd Dalton, from Louisiana, Edible offers cuisine for those with an open mind. As well as boiled rattlesnake, the restaurant offers culinary delicacies such as rattlesnake chilli and alligator stew. Why not finish a romantic meal for two with some chocolate-covered scorpions?

If you spy a fly in your soup, just count yourself lucky that you didn't order piranha fish and chips, or beer-battered locusts!

Chef Dan Craven boils a rattlesnake to make a rattlesnake chilli.

Eating his Words

As a stunt to launch the 2005 edition of This Diary Will Change Your Life, 22-year-old Londoner Will Parkinson took the wacky diary's advice to "eat this book" literally!

Helped by other ingredients, such as bread, jam, banana and vanilla milkshakes, beetroot, tomato ketchup, and coke, Will successfully consumed the entire book in seven hours!

A Cracking Idea

Competitors in the 4th of July sidewalk egg fry at Oatman, Arizona, cook eggs on the sidewalk using just the heat of the midday sun.

Champion Chomper

Sonya Thomas, aged 36, of Alexandria, Virginia, only joined the International Federation of Competitive Eating in 2003, but the 105-lb (48-kg) rookie has already set records. These include eating 8.4 lb (3.8 kg) of baked beans in under three minutes, 167 chicken wings in 32 minutes, 11 lb (5 kg) of cheesecake in nine minutes, 65 eggs in under seven minutes, 38 lobsters in 12 minutes, and 432 oysters in ten minutes.

Hot Favorite

Chicago-based Vienna Beef unveiled a 37-ft 2-in (11-m) long hot dog at the 2004 Taste of Chicago festival. The monster wiener was garnished with 1 gal (4 l) of mustard, 1 gal (4 l) of green relish, 140 tomato slices, 4 lb (2 kg) of chopped onions, and 70 pickle spears.

Cutting the Carbs

Jack LaLanne, 90, regarded by many as "the godfather of fitness," still works out for two hours a day, seven days a week. Ever since the age of 15, LaLanne has eaten a diet high in fruits and vegetables. Apparently, he hasn't had a sugary dessert since 1929.

Fruity Heirloom

Some families pass down jewelry from generation to generation, but Margie Clark of Oklahoma, is giving her kids a shrivelled orange. The shrunken, rock-hard, nearly petrified piece of fruit has been in her family since 1921 when it was given to her father by his sister, then stored in a trunk.

WHAT'S THE BEEF?

- When the first McDonald's opened in Russia, in 1990, more than 20,000 Muscovites queued to sample the wares

- The first hamburgers in the U.S.A. were served in New Haven, Connecticut, at Louis' Lunch sandwich shop in 1895. Owner Louis Lassen didn't like to waste excess beef, so he ground it, grilled it, and served it between two slices of bread

- There are an average of 178 sesame seeds on a McDonald's Big Mac bun

- In 1982, the town of Rutland, North Dakota, made a 3,591 lb (1,629 kg) hamburger, which was eaten by approximately 8,000 people

- In 1968, the Big Macs cost 49 cents (25 pence)

Wonder Drugs

Inventor Ray Kurzweil, 56, takes 250 nutritional supplements a day. Why? He wants to live longer. Kurzweil believes that he is reprogramming his body to slow down the aging process. Maybe he's on to something: he claims that tests done by a Denver clinic show that his body resembles that of a man in his early forties.

Beef it Up

Clint Stephenson, an engineer from Texas, won the Sutter Home Wineries' 2004 Build a Better Burger Contest. His winner was a grilled California Avocado B.L.T. Burger with Caramelized Chipotle Onions and blue cheese spread. He plans to build a house with his $50,000 (£26,000) prize money.

What a Whopper

What is believed to be the world's biggest commercially available burger is on sale for $23.95 (£12) at Denny's Beer Barrel Pub in Clearfield, Pennsylvania. It weighs in at a mighty 6 lb (3 kg) and Denny's claim that no customer has ever managed to finish it.

Internal Affairs

Donald Lerman lives up to his nickname of "The Beef." A stocky 5 ft 8 in (1.73 m) tall and weighing 185 lb (84 kg), in 2001 he broke the world burger speed-eating record by wolfing down 11 and a bit quarterpounders in ten minutes. Donald prepares for eating competitions by drinking up to 1 gal (4 l) of water at a time.

Pumpkin Paddlers

AN UNUSUAL CONTEST, is held annually in Nova Scotia, Canada—the pumpkin paddling regatta.

Every year, hundreds of water-loving gourd-enthusiasts compete in the race, which is held in Ladysmith Harbour. A local pumpkin grower, Howard Dill, raises a giant breed of pumpkin, called Giant Atlantic,

The regatta organizers recommend racing in pumpkins that weigh more than 600 lb (272 kg).

and rather than wasting the hollowed-out flesh after selling the seeds, gives them to contestants of the regatta so that they can further shape them to their own requirements. Not only do contestants have to bring their own wetsuits in order to compete, they must also carve out the insides to create a cockpit.

Experienced pumpkin paddler Chip Peterson dons a helmet made out of a pumpkin.

Pull Some Strings

Made using 18 gal (45 l) of olive oil, 1,100 lb (500 kg) of flour, and 1,800 eggs, this fettuccine took the record in 1997 as the world's longest noodle in Singapore. Forty chefs spent five days in the kitchen cooking up the record-breaking pasta.

The hard work of the chefs and their assistants resulted in a staggering 3,776 ft (1,151 m) of the super strings!

Snail's Pace

A French seaweed collector retained one of the world's lesser-known sporting titles in August 2004—that of champion snail-spitter. Alain Jourden, aged 43, beat off 110 rivals from 14 different countries by propelling the live mollusk 30.8 ft (9.4 m) from a running start. Despite winning, however, he failed to match his own existing world record of 34.1 ft (10.4 m) because of some adverse wind conditions on the Brittany coast.

Pride of Lions

During their annual pancake festival in 2002, members of the Lubbock Lions Club in Lubbock, Texas, made 30,724 pancakes in just eight hours.

Red Alert

Nicholas Huenefeld of Ohio can swallow 24 oz (680 g) of ketchup in one sitting.

Carton Character

Anthony Key from Bath, England, created a sculpture called Female Buddha *using only chinese takeaway cartons!*

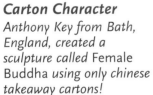

Sausage Feat

A village in Northern Serbia displayed a 3,280-ft (1,011-m) long sausage during a traditional meat festival in 1997.

Baker's Oven
Ivan "Chamouni" Chalbert baked more than bread in his 400° F (200°C) oven! The 19th century Russian baker could withstand the same heat that thoroughly cooked raw meat.

U.S.A.
Arizona

In Tombstone, it's illegal for men and women over the age of 18 to have less than one missing tooth visible when smiling.

BAKER IRON WORKS
LOS ANGELES

Ripley's®
"CHAMOUNI" THE BAKER
EXHIBIT NO: 1106
COULD CLIMB INSIDE HIS OWN OVEN AT
EXTREMELY HIGH TEMPERATURES

97

Sidewalk Show

KURT WENNER PAINTS just like one of the old masters—except he usually creates his masterpieces on the sidewalk.

Raised in Santa Barbara, California, his first job was as a space illustrator for NASA. Kurt left to study the Renaissance masters in Rome, Italy. There, he first came across a street painter, who told him all about this growing European tradition. Kurt then spent many years on his knees creating masterpieces in pastels—come rain or shine. Now a master street painter he only performs at festivals, but still loves his art. "I'm not disappointed when the painting washes away," he says, "because street painting is performance art—it's like attending a symphony."

Kurt's paintings, like this one of Echo and Narcissus, *created at the Utah Arts Festival in Salt Lake City, can last between a couple of days and a year, depending on the sidewalk and the weather.*

"Rain is the great enemy of street painters," according to Kurt, but he uses a camera to record his paintings, such as this original composition, Saint Francis Preaches to the Fish, *which he painted in his home town of Santa Barbara, California.*

Up to 500 artists make a living from street painting around the world, but Kurt no longer performs for money. He takes commissions for oil paintings, and creates street art for festivals such as the Festa Italiana in Portland, Oregon, where he painted this Merchant of Venice.

Right on Cue

At just seven years old, Landon Shuffett of Greensburg, Kentucky, has already won more than 30 adult pool tournaments. He can even sink 16 consecutive shots in a set zigzag formation.

As Easy as A, B, C

Landon is a master of the trick shot. He can clear the table from the break, and is the only player in the world who can do a "stack of two"—sinking the bottom ball of a stack without disturbing the top ball.

TATTOO YOU

- Tattooing is thought to have originated in Egypt
- The first tattoo shop opened in New York City in 1870
- Michael Wilson (the "Illustrated Man") left his native California in 1980 because tattooists there had refused to color his face
- Sixteen percent of Americans have at least one tattoo
- There are 15,000 tattoo parlors in the U.S.A.
- According to Internet search engine Lycos, "tattoos" was the third most popular search term in 2002
- An American calling himself Larry da Leopard is covered with 665 tattoos that make him look like a leopard

The Ugly Truth

Jian Feng of Hegang, northern China, was suspicious when his wife gave birth to an ugly baby. Then his wife confessed—not to adultery, but to having undergone major plastic surgery before she met him. He promptly divorced her and sued her for fraud.

Check Mate

Matt Gone is a walking, talking checkerboard. Since 1990, the New Orleans dishwasher has had 300 hours of tattoo sessions, at $44,000 (£23,000), to cover his body in black-and-white squares. The design, conceived to hide unsightly birthmarks, now covers 94 percent of Matt's body. Only his face, hands, and the soles of his feet are untouched. For variety, one leg is covered with water designs, the other with images of fire. "I see it as an art form," he says. "I'm wearing my portfolio."

Sweaty Socks

A pair of Canadian rock star Bryan Adams' sweaty socks sold for over $1,000 (£530) on eBay. Adams accidentally left the black Armani socks behind when changing for a concert but gave permission for the unwashed footwear to be sold.

Smile Please

Toothless police officers in the Philippines were issued free dentures in 2005 as part of a drive to encourage them to smile more!

What a Picture

Paul Morris paid more than £10,000 ($19,000) to have the whole of his upper body and head tattooed.

You've Gotta Hand it to Him

Vietnam veteran Bob Wieland is a regular competitor in U.S. marathons—even though he has no legs. Bob covers the 26 mi (42 km) on his hands, using a special pair of "hand shoes," made of gel and attached by leather straps. Brave Bob propelled only by his hands, crossed America in three years, eight months and six days in the 1980s. He admits it's hard going, and says: "One mile on your hands is like 25 miles on your legs."

Heavens Above!
While hanging out her washing one day, Pauline Aguss of Suffolk, England, was hit on the arm by a falling meteorite.

Nail Polish
Los Angeles anthropologist Kathy Hayes has toenails that are nearly 5 in (13 cm) long. It took her five years to grow them to that length and she considers them to be a work of art, so she keeps them sculpted and immaculately painted. The downside is that she has to wear platform sandals to prevent her nails from scraping on the ground.

The Human Slate
Rosa Barthelme was known as "the Human Slate" because she could etch words into the skin on her back, which would stay there for several minutes.

Fastest Finger
Hairdresser Valentino LoSauro, of Fort Myers, Florida, is a real-life Scissorhands. He has invented a device called "Clawz," which consists of ten mini razors attached to his fingertips. Since the contraption allows each finger to cut independently, he can do the work of ten hairdressers and saves considerable time.

They've got the Hump
The first international camel beauty pageant was held in Mongolia in 2003. Herders rated camels on their humps and the shine of their hair.

The Milky Way
Ilker Yilmaz, from Turkey, can squirt milk from his eye as far as 110 in (280 cm).

U.S.A. Minnesota
It is illegal to sleep naked.

SMiLe!

F ANCY FLASHING those pearly whites to reveal an artistic touch?

Tooth art could have you smiling to show off your pretty premolars after art dentist Ron Grant has had a chance to work his artistic magic in your mouth.

Illustrations can include patriotic flying flags, famous icons and celebrities, or pay homage to your favorite musicians and bands.

Eye Eye
If adorning your teeth isn't your thing, perhaps eye art might be. Eyeball jewelry will have people gazing into your eyes!

Body Talks

New Yorker Joe Tamargo sells advertising space—on his body. Bringing a whole new meaning to "product placement," he makes money by allowing companies to promote their wares on his body in the form of permanent tattoos. His first sale was to a Californian pharmaceutical company who paid $500 (£265) for an advertising tattoo on his right arm. He says of his new enterprise: "I figure instead of people wearing a Tommy Hilfiger logo on their shirt, they can wear the actual logo on their arm."

Licked into Shape

German schoolgirl Annika Irmler reckons that, at 3 in (7 cm), her tongue is the longest in the world. She can even lick ice-cream from the bottom of a cone while her friends have to use their fingers.

It's a Cover-up

Toronto Blue Jays pitcher Justin Miller was told to cover up the multicolored tattoos on his left arm after umpires ruled that they were a distraction to hitters.

Shorn Down

The government of North Korea has waged war on men with long hair, calling them unhygienic and "blind followers of bourgeois lifestyle." Under the new regulations men must wear their hair no longer than 2 in (5 cm), the only concession being to old men who can grow it up to 3 in (7 cm) to cover baldness. Violators risk being named and shamed on TV.

You Are What You Eat
New York played host to Rich Varano's sculpture of President George W. Bush, sculpted from an unusual material—hummus!

Glowing Praise

San Francisco tattoo artist Greg Kulz uses homemade tattoo ink to give people tattoos that glow in the dark.

Double Booking!

Canadian police officer Chris Legere booked identical twins for speeding on the same day—in the same car! One morning in January 2005 he pulled over an 18-year-old woman from Akwesasne for driving at 96 mph (154 km/h). Then in the afternoon he stopped the same car doing 92 mph (148 km/h) in the opposite direction. He first thought it was the same driver but identity checks showed it was her twin sister.

Tall Order

A club for Indian men over 6 ft (1.8 m) tall announced in 2003 that it was opening its doors to women because members have difficulty finding brides. In a country where the average male height is 5 ft 7 in (1.7 m), the club in the southern state of Kerala has attracted some 300 members. One says: "Tall people are just a laughing-stock in India. In cinema halls, we have to insist on back rows. On buses, we can't even stand properly."

Skull and Order

In a landmark operation, surgeons in Golden, Colorado, have fitted teenager Mandy Kemp with a prosthetic jaw. Mandy, who suffers from Goldenhar Syndrome, a rare genetic disorder that leaves the face looking lopsided, was fitted with a cobalt-chromium implant after 3-D imaging was used to create an exact replica of her skull and facial bones.

Four Eyes

A two-headed goat was born in Bauta, Cuba, in May 2004. Its owner, Juan Bolanos, reported that the goat could breathe and feed with both heads, and opened and closed all four of its eyes at the same time!

On Your Marx

In May 2003, 800 students and faculty members at East Lansing High School, Michigan, gathered for the biggest-ever Groucho Marx tribute. They all wore sets of Groucho glasses, fuzzy eyebrows, and moustaches.

You're Busted
In 2004, sculptor Rich Varano molded busts of presidential candidates John Kerry and George Bush out of hummus.

Fan Male

Chris Gennaro, 31, gave up a career as a doctor—so he could dress like Madonna! His obsession began when he saw the dress for 1984's "Like a Virgin". Since giving up medicine, he has worked as a waiter, and spent his time and $100,000 (£53,000) going to see Madonna and recreating 100 of her outfits on the sewing-machine in his Brooklyn apartment.

BRA-VO

- One of the first bras was made from two handkerchiefs tied together with ribbons

- In 2003, Pascal Mouawad designed a bra with 6,000 white diamonds, sapphires, amethysts, and as a centerpiece, the 70-carat Excelsior diamond. The bra was valued at $11 million (£6 million)

- Madonna's famous "Bullet Bra," which she wore during her "Blonde Ambition" tour of 1990, was modelled after an antique breastplate that was worn by Italian soldiers

Going to Pieces

The Enigma, for many years a member of The Jim Rose Circus, has his entire body covered with a blue jigsaw-puzzle tattoo. To complete his highly individual look, the American performer has also had horns implanted in the skin surrounding his skull!

Piped Music

In the 1930s, Charles Gregory, half of popular vaudeville act Gregory and Damon, played popular dance tunes on a Eureka vacuum cleaner—no other make would do.

Ducking Out

A Sao Paulo prisoner who tried to escape from jail dressed as a woman was caught because he couldn't walk in high heels. Guards at Taquaritinga Prison said Moacir Pacagnan looked like a pretty woman but waddled like a duck.

Seeing is Believing

German businessman Ralph Anderl has invented a unique pair of spectacles—"Sushi Specs." The unusual glasses have detachable arms that can be used as chopsticks!

True or False?

While fishing at Appling, Georgia, 70-year-old Verdell James sneezed violently and watched in horror as his $300 (£160) false teeth dropped into Thurmond Lake. Police rescue divers returned them two days later.

Hair Apparent

In the annual contest to find the longest beard and moustache, held in Italy, categories include freestyle, goatee, imperial, English, and Garibaldi. The use of artificial styling aids, including moustache wax, hairspray, hair gel, and styling cream, is strictly forbidden.

Hans Naumann holds the trophy for the longest moustache in the European Contest of Beards and Moustaches. At 5 ft (1.5 m) long, his 'tache was a real winner.

The Mane Attraction

Known as "Lionel the Lion-faced Boy," Stephen Bilgraski was born in Russia in the mid-19th century, and later performed in the U.S.A. with Barnum and Bailey's circus. He claimed his condition was caused by his mother seeing his father killed by a lion while she was pregnant, but we now know it was due to a rare genetic disorder called hypertrichosis or werewolf syndrome.

The Boy Who Never Grew Up

Randy Constin lives in his own Never Never Land. The 50-year-old from Britain is so obsessed with Peter Pan that for the past 30 years he has worn green tights. His fixation, which includes climbing trees and leaping from them in a bid to emulate his hero, has seen him lose both his wife and his job. "Being Peter Pan is part of my life," he says. "When I was eight I told my dad I wanted to be a fairy."

Stretch Your Legs

Teenager Emma Richards from Cornwall, England, underwent a six-hour operation in 2000 to have her legs stretched. She wanted to increase her height from 4 ft 9 in (1.45 m) to 5 ft 2 in (1.6 m) so that she could achieve her ambition of becoming a flight attendant.

Window Pain

Tattoo artist Miranda Griffiths of Washington, D.C., sports self-designed tattoos of stained-glass windows on her lower legs.

Rogue Mail

Here's proof that Bill Clinton didn't think much of online correspondence during his presidency—he sent only two e-mails during his entire term in office. In comparison, his staff sent just under 40 million. One of his e-mails was to test the system, while the second was sent to astronaut John Glenn to congratulate him on his return to space. Both e-mails are now archived in the Bill Clinton Presidential Library.

He Spoke Too Soon

At the Phuket Vegetarian Festival in Thailand, pierced participants parade through the streets to show their devotion to their religion. Their piercings are adorned with objects including swords, skewers, branches —and even a bicycle.

RuNS in the FaMiLy

FAST AND FUNNY is always the order of the day for Fran Capo and her son Spencer Patterson.

If living with Fran, the world's fastest-talking woman, would be enough to drive you mad, then at least Spencer, the world's youngest comic, could perhaps help you to see the funny side of things.

Inspired by his mother, Spencer Patterson dared to brave the stage himself, and became the world's youngest comic at the age of two. His career to date has seen him appear in a host of movies, and on various radio and television shows as both a comedian and ventriloquist.

Fran Capo talked her way into the record books when she first appeared on the Larry King Live show in 1986, speaking at an amazing 585 words per minute! She also became the first author to hold a book signing at the top of Mount Kilimanjaro, Africa.

Apatani Tradition
The Apatani women of India traditionally wore nose plugs in their nostrils. However, this custom is now in decline, as is the wearing of their traditional dress and necklaces.

Snakes Alive
The latest trend among New York society women is to carry live snakes as an accessory! The snakes are usually carried in handbags and are chosen for their color—green garters and bright-banded corn snakes are particularly popular.

Ear, Ear
Many a man is proud of his long hair, but B.D. Tyagi of Bhopal, India, rejoices at the length of his ear hair. Wild and wiry, it sprouts an amazing 4 in (10 cm) from his outer ear.

Center Forward
Pregnant women who like to show off their bellies have a firm ally in American artist Laurie Steinfeld. He makes sure their expanded bellies really do stand out by painting them to resemble soccer balls or basketballs.

Tough Talk
Who says Klingons can't spread peace? On *Star Trek* they are short-tempered thugs who live for battle, but San Diego Trekkies known as "the Imperial Klingon Vessel Stranglehold" visit schools dressed in full Klingon garb to talk about how to solve squabbles. They believe kids can learn from the culture's strict code of honor.

All Fingers and Toes
In the 1920s, all the villagers in Cervera de Buitrago, Spain, had extra digits.

Bottle Neck

Circus of Horrors performer Satanica can fit into a bottle as part of her act with Docktor Haze.

Bouncing Baby

Born in Boston, Massachusetts, early last century, Diamond Kitty weighed 92 lb (42 kg) at just six months of age. She grew up to become a circus sideshow "fat lady," and weighed more than 600 lb (272 kg).

Shake a Leg

David Spinler, a farmer from Freeborn County, Minnesota, had been told by the vet to expect his cow to have twin calves in 2004. Instead, there was just one calf, but it had an extra two legs protruding from its back. Sadly, the six-legged animal died during birth, but David was so intrigued by it that he decided to have it preserved by a taxidermist.

U.S.A. Alabama

It is illegal to wear a fake moustache that causes laughter in church.

Green Fingers

When a four-year-old Romanian boy went for a routine check-up in 2003, doctors found a plant growing from his nose! The boy, from a mountain village, hadn't complained about the bean, which even had little leaves.

Guilty Secret

A man from Long Beach, California, was convicted of armed robbery in 2003 after being identified by tattoos including a gun on his neck and the words "not guilty."

Playing Hard Ball
Alex Ednie had a super-strong golf swing—he could shoot balls right through a phone book!

Ringing the Changes
With more than 230 piercings, Cuba's Luis Antonio Aguero is the world's most pierced man.

Knife and Fork

Seth Griffin speaks with a forked tongue—literally. A friend used a scalpel to split the tongue of the 29-year-old body-piercer from Bay City, Michigan. He also has three Teflon domes implanted in his chest, and more than 30 piercings on his body, including the bridge of his nose, his eyebrows, nipples, lips, septum, and ears. "It's not a fashion statement," says Seth with a slight lisp. "It's about feeling good about myself. I feel I am different from other people, so I set myself apart by changing the way I look."

Making a Point

A Chinese man has had plastic surgery to give him pointed ears like *Star Trek*'s Mr. Spock. The young man astonished surgeons in Nanjing when he told them he wanted alien-like ears because he was bored with their current shape. Despite their misgivings, the surgeons decided to go ahead with the operation.

A School for Santas

The "Ministry of Fun Santa School" in London, England, hosted a training day to enable professional Santa Claus performers to fine-tune their festive duties!

Pins and Needles

Brent Moffatt has turned himself into a human pincushion. In December 2003, Moffatt, who lives in Moose Jaw, Saskatchewan, inserted 900 surgical needles into his leg simultaneously. This amazing total easily surpassed his previous record of 702 body piercings. Although Brent admits that there were a few trickles of blood, he insisted that he felt no pain. "It just felt like a whole bunch of little ants crawling over me," he declared stoically.

Let Your Hair Down

After 38 years without a haircut, Tran Van Hay from Vietnam has hair more than 20.3 ft (6.2 m) in length!

Spelling Test

Lee Williams of Roseville, Michigan, sued a tattoo parlor for $25,000 (£13,000) in 1999 for misspelling a tattoo on his right forearm. The word "villain" came out as "villian" because neither Williams nor the tattooist knew how to spell it.

SPLIT ENDS

- On average, we lose between 30 and 60 hairs every day

- A single hair can hold the weight of a large apple

- If all the eyelashes you shed in your life were joined together, they would form a strand more than 100 ft (30 m) long

- Human eyelashes are shed after about 150 days

- In the course of an average lifetime, you will grow 6 ft (1.8 m) of nose hair

- There are 30,000 whiskers on the face of the average man

- François I of France hated beards so much that he made the wearing of them punishable by death

Can't StoMach It!

STRONGMAN Jess Caigoy is known as the Human Vacuum Cleaner!

Jess feasts on a variety of unpalatable items, including worms and grubs, washes them all down, and then regurgitates them using a long tube stuck down his throat.

Jess inserts the tube after he's feasted enough!

Jess starts by helping himself to a range of unusual appetizers!

He throws his head back to make sure they go down.

He washes them down.

Jess prepares for the regurgitation by passing the tube down his throat.

115

Couch-bound

Gayle Grinds, a 400 lb (180 kg) Florida woman, died in 2004 after emergency workers tried to remove her from the couch where she had spent the previous six years.

Hair and Now

Officially China's hairiest man, Yu Zhenhuan's body is 96 percent covered in hair. Twenty-six-year-old Yu recently underwent surgery to remove some hair from his ear, which had caused hearing loss. Doctors believe he has an average of 41 hairs per 0.15 sq in (1 sq cm).

Hold Your Horses

Cosmetic tattoo artist Teri Reid is used to a wide variety of customers, but she never expected to tattoo a horse! As a break from her usual clientele, Teri, from Twin Falls, Idaho, treats American paint horses whose pale coats leave little natural pigmentation around the eyes. When they are exposed to sunlight, the glare can cause serious eye problems. So Teri puts the horses under anesthetic and applies permanent black eyeliner.

"It's like giving a horse a pair of sunglasses," she says.

Bearded Lady

Set up by computer programmer Jerry Jackson, the Internet's National Beard Registry features over 250 hairy Americans. Jerry wanted the site to show that it's OK to grow facial hair, no matter what the boss thinks. In 2004, the first whiskered woman joined—a 26-year-old from Philadelphia with a short brown goatee that she had been growing for just over a year.

Swine Fever

Norwegian pig farmer Arne Braut has started wearing a pig mask and grunting at his swine in the hope of forging a closer relationship. He claims that they are much calmer when they think he is another pig.

A Bit of Fluff

Priscella, known as "Monkey Girl," had a completely hairy body and a full beard. She was married to circus performer "Emmett, the alligator skinned man," and together they performed with the Calvacade of Amusements at Coney Island in the 1920s.

Hair Style

A Romanian woman makes clothes from her own hair! Ioana Cioanca has been saving every hair that falls out for nearly 50 years, ever since her grandmother told her it was a sin to throw it away. She now has an entire wardrobe of hair fashion, including a raincoat, waistcoat, blouse, skirt, hat, and a matching handbag.

Picture This

Julia Gnuse of Los Angeles, California, began tattooing her body in 1991 in order to conceal the effects of a rare skin condition. She is now tattooed from the top of her head right down to her ankles—including her face and fingers mainly with figures from television and the movies.

Human Kebabs

Worshipers in Malaysia celebrate at the annual Thaipusam festival near Kuala Lumpur by hooking and sticking skewers through their own skin to the accompaniment of deafening music that apparently helps to ease the pain.

My Left Feet

Japanese police arrested 45-year-old Ichiro Irie in October 2003—after 440 women's left shoes were found in his home. "I have always been interested in women's feet," he explained to police. They remained baffled, however, about his preference for left feet.

He's for the Chop

On October 16, 2004, the unbelievable strength of karate instructor Mike Reeves was proved yet again when, in front of the Ripley Museum in Orlando, he broke 1,534 1-in (2.5-cm) thick boards in just 10 minutes and 12 seconds.

Fat Cat

In August 2004, Dr. Robert Ersek, who is better known as "the biggest fat-sucker in Austin, Texas," performed liposuction in front of television cameras—on himself! The American plastic surgeon performed this feat as part of his program of promoting the potential use of stem cells, which can be harvested in such operations. As the 66-year-old sucked fat cells out of his belly, he said: "We're doing our part to keep Austin weird."

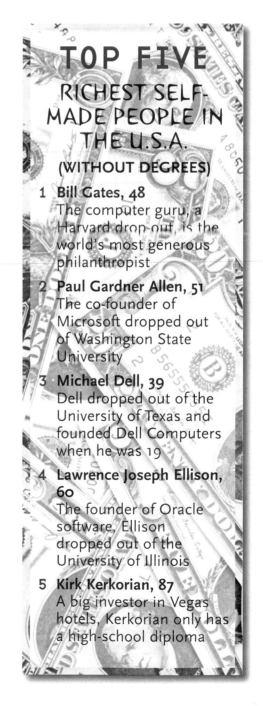

TOP FIVE
RICHEST SELF-MADE PEOPLE IN THE U.S.A.
(WITHOUT DEGREES)

1 **Bill Gates, 48**
The computer guru, a Harvard drop-out, is the world's most generous philanthropist

2 **Paul Gardner Allen, 51**
The co-founder of Microsoft dropped out of Washington State University

3 **Michael Dell, 39**
Dell dropped out of the University of Texas and founded Dell Computers when he was 19

4 **Lawrence Joseph Ellison, 60**
The founder of Oracle software, Ellison dropped out of the University of Illinois

5 **Kirk Kerkorian, 87**
A big investor in Vegas hotels, Kerkorian only has a high-school diploma

Hero Worship

Belgian Emmanuel de Reyghere has had nine operations to make him look like Michael Jackson. "Some people spend their money on golf," he says. "I just spend all my money on making my face look like Michael's." His girlfriend left him five years ago.

Blooming Marvellous

U.S. hair-stylist Kevin Carter, from Southfield, Michigan, is renowned for his ability to turn hair into floral arrangements. At Hair Wars 2000, in Detroit, he spent nearly three hours turning a model into a vase for a 2-ft (0.6-m) high sansevieria plant made of hair. First he stitched the plant to a fabric base that was stitched to the model's hair, then he combed and sprayed her hair so that it blended into the plant.

The Boy with Two Brains

An Afghan woman gave birth to a two-headed boy in Iran in August 2004. Najmeh Wahedian's son was born by Caesarian section with an apparently normal body, but with two separate heads on his shoulders. Medical tests showed that the baby had two functioning brains, each controlling one side of the body, two hearts, and two spinal cords. Sometimes one head cried while the other slept.

FASHION VICTIMS

- Fashion followers in the 18th century wore false eyebrows made from mouse skin
- In 16th-century Italy, it was the fashion for women to color their teeth
- Men didn't wear underwear until the 16th century
- Spain's Prince Philip of Calabria loved gloves so much that he often wore 16 pairs at a time
- Queen Victoria was amused to be given a novelty bustle that played "God Save the Queen" when she sat down

Bra Constrictor

Customs officers in Stockholm, Sweden, arrested a woman who tried to smuggle 75 live snakes in her bra. The officers were suspicious as the woman kept scratching her chest.

Chainsaw Art

Carroll Sanders of Hawesville, Kentucky, risks life and limb to carve letters on to his toenails—using a full-size chainsaw.

Goodness Nose

A campaign launched in Los Angeles in 2002 included a "Show off your Nose" contest, in which noses of all shapes and sizes were measured and recorded.

New Moon

In 1934 Clyde Van Patten, an evangelist from Michigan, attracted massive crowds to hear his sermons. The reason for the wide attraction was because he promised to perform songs—using just his nose.

Record Achievement

At just 27.9 in (70.9 cm) tall, Bryan Naranjo, 18, is one of the shortest men in South America.

Lady Gray

Rosemary Jacobs, from Atlanta, Georgia, has a rare skin condition called argyria, which has turned her skin gray. She thinks it's due to nose drops she took as a child, which contained silver. Flakes of silver have been found in her skin.

Turtle Mutates

Michele Ivey of Ferndale, Michigan, sees herself as the fifth Ninja Turtle. At the age of 11, she fell in love with Michelangelo, the green-masked party dude of the Teenage Mutant Ninja Turtles, and she's spent the past 15 years chasing her obsession. In that time she has spent $5,000 (£2,700) on karate lessons, and has even bought a replica head of Michelangelo to wear. She says the turtles give her inner strength.

U.S.A.
Arizona

Donkeys are not permitted to sleep in bathtubs.

I.D. Tag

T.D. Rockwell, from San Francisco had his own name and address—as well as that of his bank—tattooed on his leg in 27 languages, including Morse Code and semaphore.

Double Trouble

A ten-year-old boy got the shock of his life in 2003 when he stumbled across a two-headed snake. Hunter York of Centertown, Kentucky, took the non-venomous king snake home to look after it, but his family didn't know which head to feed.

A Full Moon

Railroad passengers going through Laguna Niguel, California, on the second Saturday in July always see a full moon. In a bizarre annual ceremony, hundreds of drinkers from the nearby Mugs Away Saloon drop their trousers and bare their bottoms at the 25 trains that pass through that day. It began in 1979, when K.T. Smith offered to buy a drink for anyone willing to moon the next train. Moon Amtrak is now so popular that for that Saturday trains are booked solid for months in advance.

Delicate Touch

Indian micro-artist Anoop Bhalla paints or writes on grains of food, such as this grain of rice.

What a Catch

Al Green of the Bronx, New York, caught 26 foul balls at Brooklyn Dodgers games in 1946. Over the next four years, he caught 211 balls at Dodgers, Giants, and Yankees games. Al worked nights and so could go to both afternoon and evening games.

PaiNted LadY

Body artists were able to capture the mythical theme using various techniques.

BODY-PAINTERS FROM all over the world flocked to Austria in 2004 to see the many wonders on display.

The World Body-Painting Festival ran a myths, fairy tales, and water theme, which resulted in some spectacular sights and a magical atmosphere.

Half human, half alien, using body paint, costumes, and accessories only.

Choc Full
On February 14, 1997, chocoholics Melanie Lugo and Kevin Kuhlman tied the knot while sitting in a bathtub that had been filled with cooled liquid chocolate. The couple, who were married by Reverend Stern, arranged for a restaurant in New York to prepare the chocolate in advance.

TOP FIVE
SALE ITEMS AT MADONNA'S 2001 AUCTION

1 **Dolce and Gabbana bra** (1993 "Girlie" tour) $23,850 (£12,650)

2 **Black sequined bra** (1987 "Who's That Girl" tour) $20,550 (£10,900)

3 **John Galliano suit** ("Take a Bow" video) $13,800 (£7,300)

4 **Jean-Paul Gaultier lace gown** $11,200 (£5,950)

5 **Black-and-gold beaded gloves** (1987 "Who's That Girl" tour) $7,000 (£3,700)

On Ice
In 1989, Tygve Bauge, a resident of Nederland, Colorado, had the body of his dead grandfather shipped from Norway and packed in ice in a shed so that he could resurrect him in the future. Tygve was subsequently deported, but Grandpa Bredo was allowed to remain in Nederland and, although his body has not been seen for some years, his presence is celebrated by the town each March on Frozen Dead Guy Day. Events include a coffin race, a snow-sculpting contest, Grandpa lookalike competitions, and guided tours to the shed.

A Twist in the Nail
India's Romesh Sharma shows off his fingernails, which are a staggering 33 ft (10 m) long. Romesh's talons set a new world record in New Delhi in 2003 easily breaking the previous record of 20.18 ft (6.15 m).

U.S.A.
Federal

No person may appear as a contestant on more than one game show each year.

Telly Addicts

Vivian Weiss and Joseph Pepper were both residents in the same city in Nebraska. However, they had more in common than they realized: after often being mistaken for each other, they met at a party, where they discovered that they not only shared a birthday, but also an anniversary, stomach complaints, had children of similar ages and liked and disliked the same foods!

Modern Art is Rubbish

Sculptor Rick Carpenter is the 43rd artist to hold the title "Artist in Residence" at San Francisco's Solid Waste Transfer and Recycling Center, which is otherwise known as the city dump. Every artist brings their own specialty to the position. Carpenter says that he is creating art from discarded bulk items, and cites the weaving he made from 40 orange extension cords.

Top That

The longest beard chain in the world was created by two men called Chervalier and Schaffer in Stuttgart, Germany. Twenty bearded participants tied their beards together, creating the longest beard chain ever recorded— 78.7 ft (24 m)!

Wind Bags

Some people will buy anything from eBay. Recent bidders agreed to pay $10 (£5) for wind "captured" from Hurricane Frances and stored in Tupperware containers.

The Missing Links

In the 1930s, Mrs. Jake Hamon of Ardmore, Oklahoma, had her husband's diamond cuff links made into a stick pin that she wore in her pierced throat.

Bald is Beautiful

Ever since he started losing his hair at 15, John Capps has believed that bald is beautiful. He is clearly not alone as his society, Bald Headed Men of America, boasts over 35,000 members. Each year, they meet in Morehead City, North Carolina, for the Bald is Beautiful Convention. As Capps says: "Morehead means less hair."

Plastic Fantastic

The world's first beauty contest solely for women who have undergone plastic surgery took place in China in 2004. Contestants for Miss Plastic Surgery had to produce a doctor's certificate confirming that their charms weren't natural. One entrant had undergone no fewer than 13 operations.

Payment in Kind

When Don, a well known San Francisco panhandler, recently inherited $187,000 (£99,300) from his estranged mother, he gave $10,000 (£5,000) to the Blue Room Gallery. He had sat in front of the art gallery for two years begging for food and money, and wanted to pay the staff back for being nice to him.

EYES DOWN

- Human eyes are composed of more than 2 million working parts

- The eye can process 36,000 pieces of information an hour

- In a normal lifespan, you will process almost 24 million images of the world around you

- Women blink nearly twice as often as men

- Every time you blink, you close your eyes for 0.1 second, which means your eyes are closed for at least 30 minutes a day just from blinking

- A typical broadsheet newspaper issue contains about 100,000 words. In order to read every one of them, your eyes must travel further than 0.5 mi (1 km)

- If you go blind in one eye, you'll only lose about one-fifth of your vision

Number Crunching

Arthur Lloyd, the Human Card Index, had more than 15,000 index cards in his robe, packed with bits of trivia. He's seen here with Robert Ripley in 1936.

Cutting a Dash

Two hairdressers in India have come up with unusual ways to cut hair. Harish Bhatia can create six different styles while blindfolded, and Aqueel Kiratpuri uses a tiny candle flame to give his customers a porcupine look which he calls the "Candle Cut."

Harish Bhatia runs classes for visually impaired people who want to be hairdressers.

A customer sits very still while Aqueel Kiratpuri demonstrates his unique "Candle Cut."

Rope Warrior

J UMPING ROPE HAS never been quite so spectacular!

David Fisher, "The Rope Warrior," makes amazing stunts look simple—like "tush-ups," jumping rope while bouncing on his behind, and dribbling a ball at the same time. Not only can he perform a great range of stunts, but he can also speed-jump at more than 100 mph (160 km/h)! David has made more than 75 television appearances. He performed at President George W. Bush's first inauguration, and attends school assemblies every week to stress the importance of teamwork and physical fitness.

"My Ropenastics program is inexpensive, portable, infinite in its creative possibilities, and is one of the best cardiovascular workouts one can get," claims David.

The Story of Omi

Omi the Tattooed Man was covered in tattoos from the top of his head to the soles of his feet. Sometimes billed as a Maori when he performed at Ripley's Odditorium in New York City in 1939, he was actually a British World War 1 recruit.

Art and Sole

You might think fishy footwear means soles and 'eels, but English designer Oliver Sweeney has created a men's shoe made from a stingray. The skin of the flat fish forms the uppers, and the shoes have a traditional leather sole. They sell for £750 ($1,400) a pair.

Super Surgeon

Lebanese doctor Ira Kahn had an inflamed appendix and was on his way to the hospital, but got stuck in a traffic jam. When he realized that it would take him too long to get to the hospital, he made a risky decision —he performed emergency surgery on himself to remove his appendix.

Something for Nothing

Ted Matthison went without food, shelter, water, sunblock—and clothes—during a recent week-long festival in the Nevada desert. Why? To gauge the kindness of others. Fortunately for Matthison, he found that people are basically generous: within hours he was given food and water, and within days he acquired a complete campsite.

Kiss and Tell

Catherine Wagner, 69, of Ohio, has finally become a member of her high school honor society. She was barred from membership 51 years ago because she was caught in the school hall kissing her boyfriend—to whom she has now been married for more than 40 years. It was only last year, at her 50th high school reunion, that the current principal learned of her snub and saw to it that she was inducted.

Keeping Quiet

In ancient China, husbands who thought that their wives talked too much could divorce them!

Back to Front

Pierre Beauchemin, of France, was more than your average contortionist—not only was he able to scratch his ears with his feet, he could also turn his legs around so that he appeared to walk backward while moving forward!

Two of a Kind

Twins Reba and Lori Schappell, 44, are incredibly close yet have never seen each other's faces without a mirror. Joined at the head, they face in opposite directions. The twins from Reading, Pennsylvania, who also have to use a mirror to watch TV together, share 30 percent of their brain tissue, as well as one non-functional eye. Yet they have managed to lead normal lives. Reba is a country singer while Lori worked part-time in a hospital laundry until she quit to support her sister's music career.

Rolling in the Aisles

It wasn't a church aisle that checkout-operator Jill Piggot went up when she married fellow supermarket worker Pete Freeman, in 2004—it was a supermarket aisle! The couple were married in the Asda store in York, England.

The supermarket-crazy couple celebrated their nuptials with a ride in a shopping cart.

U.S.A. Massachusetts

In Boston, two people may not kiss in front of a church.

A Stitch in Time

Nancy Kirk, a quilt restorer from Nebraska, is on a crusade to save an estimated 5 million damaged quilts in America by teaching her quilting skills to others. She has to move fast, as there are fewer than three dozen quilt restorers left in America.

Boogie on Down

Carolyn Gable, who owns her own transportation company in Chicago, initiated daily boogie sessions after her managers attended a motivational seminar and learned that employees are more productive with active work breaks. Employees now enjoy morning and afternoon disco breaks, and both morale and productivity are up.

Beyond the Grave

One way of handling death is to laugh at it, like the makers of these humorous headstones in Moultrie, Georgia, and at the Merry Cemetery in Sapanta, Romania.

HERE LIES THE FATHER OF 29

HE WOULD HAVE HAD MORE BUT HE DIDN'T HAVE TIME

It's a Dog's Life

YOU MAY THINK that luxury is the sole preserve of humankind, but you'd be wrong.

Now your pets can be treated to exactly the same kind of pampering as you. You can even treat them to such delights as a night in a top-quality hotel, at which they can experience a hot-spring treatment!

A hotel in Paris, France, has taken customer service to the next level. The hotel staff are all specially trained to deliver the highest-quality food and service to pets!

Pampered Pooch

Jasper, a black Doberman-Labrador, travels by stretch limo and owns stocks and shares worth £130,000 ($250,000). The dog, who lives with his owner, Sir Benjamin Slade, in Somerset, England, also enjoys a daily menu of sirloin steak, Dover sole, and New Zealand freshwater mussels.

TOP FIVE
DOG TALES

1 An estimated 1 million dogs in the U.S.A. have been named primary beneficiary in their owners' wills

2 Every dog except the chow has a pink tongue—the chow's tongue is jet black

3 Sumo, a Neapolitan mastiff, was evicted from his owner's flat in Romania in 2004 because neighbors complained that he snored too loudly

4 Each year, parks in London, England, are soaked in 1 million gal (4.5 million l) of dog urine

5 When Ella Wendel of New York died in 1931, she left $75 million (£40 million) to her poodle, Toby

Four Paw-ster
Who couldn't get a good night's sleep in a luxury four-poster bed? Evie was a lucky enough dog to spend the night in one of designer Jane Evans' luxurious bespoke doggy beds.

Bark-itecture
This state-of-the-art dog kennel, designed by architect Lisa Vogt, sold for $9,200 (£4,800) when it was auctioned for charity in Florida in 2004.

131

Chipmunk Cheek
When Charlie the chipmunk decided he was thirsty, a long, cool glass of freshly squeezed orange juice didn't last very long. Charlie deftly sucks on the straw before diving head-first into the glass and gulping the lot!

High Steaks

When Romanian health officials investigated a strange smell coming from the home of Gyenge Lajos, they discovered that the 74-year-old was storing a dead cow in his living-room! Apparently he had been given the animal by a friend and carved and cooked strips of the rotting corpse when he felt hungry.

Feline Romantic

In 1996, two rare "diamond-eyed" cats called Phet and Ploy were married in a Thai disco. The event cost $16,241 (£8,500).

This Bone's Chewy

If your dog's breath is causing offense, you need to give them chewing gum for dogs. The gum, which is made by the Brazilian company Chiclet, looks like a bone and is made from edible leather.

Oh Deer

You might be surprised to learn that the most dangerous animals at large in the United States of America are not bears, sharks, poisonous snakes, or even spiders—but deer. The mild-mannered mammals are responsible for the deaths of about 100 people every year because they often cause road accidents. Bees, dogs, rattlesnakes, and spiders also rank among the top five killers in the animal world.

Best-dressed Crab

First held in 1975, the Miss Crustacean Hermit-Crab Beauty Contest draws hundreds of enthusiasts to the beach at Ocean City, New Jersey, for the search to find the best-dressed crab. Past entries have included Cleopatra Crab and Crabzilla.

Monkey Business

Declaring that he wanted to be "at one with the monkeys," 32-year-old Peter Vetique stripped down to his boxer shorts, scaled a 6-m (20-ft) high fence and jumped into the gorilla enclosure at New York's Bronx Zoo in 2001.

Lounge Lizards

In 2002 police called to a man's apartment in Newark, Delaware, after he had failed to report for work, found his body on the floor... and his pet Nile monitor lizards feeding on his flesh.

Holy Cow!

Cats, dogs, gerbils, guinea pigs, parakeets, and a tortoise were among the congregation at the 2003 Blessing of the Animals service at Saint Philip's in the Hills Episcopal Church, Tucson, Arizona. Hundreds of owners and their pets gathered for the service, which went off peacefully apart from a beagle barking during prayers.

Suite Talk

A pet hotel in Fairfax County, Virginia, charges $230 (£120) for a dog's use of a hydrotherapy pool, state-of-the-art exercise room, beauty parlor, and suites with satellite TV and classical music.

Meowing Muse

When Marilyn, a Doberman pinscher, ran away from her new home in Sault Ste Marie, Ontario, in 2002, owners Ron and Peggy Lund lured her back using a borrowed kitten. The dog adores kittens and was powerless to resist the plaintive miaowing.

Like Headless Chickens

Commemorating a story about a chicken from the 1940s that allegedly lived for 18 months after having its head chopped off, the town of Fruita, Colorado, holds an annual "Mike the Headless Chicken Day." Events include the 3 mi (4.5 km) "Run Like a Headless Chicken Race," egg tosses, "Pin the Head on the Chicken," "Chicken Bingo," and the classic "Chicken Dance."

The Price of Luxury

Some of the priciest pets coveted by Americans cost more than a luxury car. For instance, a lavender albino ball python will set you back approximately $40,000 (£21,000), a striped ball python will cost you $20,000 (£10,500), and a reticulated albino tiger python costs $15,000 (£8,000).

On the Couch
Pam Whyte, a canine therapist from Cape Town, South Africa, has a consultation with a collie.

It's a Dog's Life

A hot spring in Tokyo, Japan, has shelled out on a new annex— designed especially for dogs! For as little as $25 (£13), pets can enjoy a hot tub filled with volcanic waters, before retiring to a luxury room for a dog nap.

Poodle Power

Palm Beach County, Florida, the scene of voting controversy during the 2000 presidential election, was at the eye of a fresh electoral row in 2001, when it emerged that Cocoa Fernandez was registered to vote. The problem was, Cocoa was a poodle belonging to 62-year-old Wendy Albert.

Building up his Mussels

A Purdue University professor has discovered how mussels stick themselves to surfaces: they attach tiny filaments to objects that act like glue. He believes that this mussel "glue" could be used commercially in the future, perhaps in sealing wounds or in nerve reconstruction.

Fir Goodness' Sake

For some reason, a dog in Denver, Colorado, scampered 30 ft (9 m) up a blue spruce tree. Amused city workers had to enlist the services of a cherry-picker to bring the poor pooch down to earth.

The Great Escape

Red is one cunning dog, but kennel owners hope his jail breaks are a thing of the past. Red's expertise, it seems, is breaking out of his cage at Battersea Dogs' Home, London, England, for midnight raids on the kitchen—and freeing the other dogs to join him. Having observed Red's technique on video, staff have added extra security devices to his kennel.

Snake in the Grass

A New Jersey man tried to steal two pythons and was bitten for his actions. The 20-year-old thief managed to slip the snakes out of a pet store in canvas bags attached to his pants. But on the drive home one of the snakes wrapped around the man's leg and latched on to his groin.

The Hitcher

A Russian Blue/Angora cross-bred cat by the name of Tracker went on an unplanned 150-mi (225-km) ride from Kalamazoo to Rochester Hills, Michigan, when Patricia Verduin, a college student, drove home for Christmas. Despite traveling under the hood, Tracker didn't seem harmed by the experience.

To Dye For...

Coloring your hair is no longer the preserve of humans. A pet grooming parlour in Chongqing, China, has started to offer services for pets including haircut and color.

MoRe ThaN You CaN Chew

A 50-LB (23-KG) FLATHEAD catfish had to be rescued after it playfully grabbed a basketball— and got it stuck in its mouth!

The catfish wrapped its jaws around the basketball, which was floating in the water, but the ball got stuck in the fish's tight grip. Pam and Bill Driver, from Wichita, Kansas, saw that the fish was in trouble and could not swim freely with the ball wedged in its mouth, and they began a brave rescue attempt.

It becomes clear to the Drivers that the catfish is in need of help, so Bill goes to the aid of the fish and gets into the water.

The ball is jammed so tightly into the catfish's mouth that it's a struggle to remove it— but it has to be done to allow the fish to swim freely again.

Bill finally manages to get hold of the catfish and pull the basketball from its tight grip.

Crocodile Priority

Patients waiting for ultrasound treatment at a hospital in Croatia were kept waiting for hours after a doctor took his 4-ft (1.2 m) pet crocodile for a check-up.

Milking it

This 1928 statue commemorates the world's champion milk-producing cow—it produced 3,739 gal (16,997 l) of milk in one of its record-beating years! It also produced 2,865 lb (1,230 kg) of butter. You can see just how many milk bottles would have been needed to contain all the milk.

Sonic Saviors

Dolphin researcher Dr. Michael Hyson says that the mammals can generate sound and electromagnetic fields that may be able to help treat human diseases. He believes they have something to contribute in the treatment of conditions such as autism, cerebral palsy, and depression. Speaking from experience, he says that a dolphin helped to heal a couple of painful dislocated vertebrae in his own back when he went swimming with the creature.

Party Animal

In 2004, British pet lover Jan Einzig threw a champagne party at a top London club for her West Highland terrier Gucci. To date, she has also spent more than £12,000 ($23,000) on vet's bills for treatments for the ailing dog.

Insect Lover

A lonely widower in Beijing, China, kept some 200,000 cockroaches in his home as pets. He began breeding them following the death of his wife.

Flight of Fancy

American entrepreneurs Mark and Lorraine Moore have been raking in big bucks by selling bird diapers through their company, the appropriately titled Avian Fashions. The Lycra suits, which cost between $20 (£10) and $26 (£14), allow pet birds to roam freely around their owner's house without soiling the furniture—that is as long as the pads are changed every six hours. The Moores say their friends and family initially thought the idea was rather "flighty."

Champion Chimp
Animals can be just as creative us humans. You only have to look at the works of art produced by Asuka, a three-year-old chimpanzee, who made her debut in the art world when she exhibited 50 of her paintings in Tokyo in 2004.

Cat People

A Georgia couple adopted 77 cats, with the Humane Society's blessing, because they take such good care of them. All of the felines are healthy, well fed, and given access to lots and lots of litter boxes. The couple go through 60 lb (27 kg) of cat litter each week.

Fat Chance

Pumpkin, who weighed 12 lb (5 kg), was certainly one chubby Chihuahua. Her Florida owner took her to the local veterinary surgeon for a little liposuction, where they removed 12 oz (340 g) of fat. However, the surgeon reminded Pumpkin's owner that in order to stay svelte, the pooch really needed to take regular exercise and wolf down fewer treats.

Café Society

The Meow Mix Café opened on Fifth Avenue in New York City in 2004. The cat clientele are offered various different Meow Mix varieties. Alternatives to cat food are available for their owners.

Do You Take Amex?

Her Highness Princess Zarina Zainal of Malaysia thinks nothing of traveling halfway around the globe to visit the vet with her 16-year-old Yorkshire terrier, Amex. Every trip involves a 14-hour flight from Bangkok to Paris, followed by a seven-hour flight from Paris to New York, and then a two-hour drive to the vet's office in South Salem, New York.

Playful Pigs

Pigs were taught to play video games and hit targets and match objects, using their snouts to control the joysticks. The feat was set-up and recorded by Prof. Curtis at Pennsylvania State University. Rewards came in the form of candies.

Ear, Ear
Jack, a two-year-old basset-hound, has ears that measure a whopping 13 in (33 cm) in length! Jack's ears are insured for $50,000 (£26,000).

Honey Bunch

Steve Conlon runs a honey business in West Virginia. The honey-bees join in Steve's unusual party piece: wearing a living "beard" of about 10,000 bees on his face!

Trick or Treat?

Michele Carlin of Michigan sells Halloween costumes for dogs from her store, the Puppy Boutique. She takes her own Yorkshire terrier and schnauzer trick-or-treating, and encourages others to do the same.

The Importance of Being Ernest's

About 60 cats live at the Ernest Hemingway Home and Museum in Key West, Florida. Most are descended from Hemingway's pet cat, Princess Six Toes.

All the Presidents' Pets

The Presidential Pet Museum in Maryland, just 20 mi (30 km) from the White House, has more than 500 items related to the pets of past presidents.

Bear-faced Cheek

Juan, an Andean spectacled bear, made a dramatic bid for freedom at Germany's Berlin Zoo in August 2004. First he paddled across a moat using a log as a raft, then he scaled the wall of his enclosure. Bizarrely, he looked to complete his getaway on a bicycle, which he found standing against the zoo railings. Before he could climb onto the saddle, he was cornered by zoo-keepers wielding brooms, and immobilized with a tranquillizer dart.

Giddy Up

Whiplash the monkey is a rodeo act with a difference—he rode in a tiny saddle on the back of a collie to herd sheep at the annual Calgary Stampede in Alberta, Canada.

In the Dog House

German police who were responding to a complaint about excessively loud noise had to force their way into a house when no one answered the door. They were surprised to find Bruno the Alsatian cross-breed sitting on the couch with his paw on the television's remote control.

Sign Here, Please

Rin Tin Tin, a German shepherd, was Hollywood's first canine star. He starred in 27 movies, always signing his contracts with paw prints. His death in 1932 made front-page news.

Packing a Punch

George W. Bush's pet Scottish terrier appeared in a spoof political video during the campaign trail for the 2004 election. Barney the dog was shown dressed in a headband and barking at Jon Kerry's dog, with the theme from the *Rocky* films playing as background music.

Marked From Birth

Why, it's a Goldfish
This goldfish, which grew up in an aquarium in Taipei, China, has birth markings of a question mark on its face.

IN AUGUST 2003, an eight-year-old boy made a happy discovery as he walked along a beach in Mie Prefecture, Japan—a crab with a smiley face on its shell!

This species of crab, ironically called *Gaetice depressus*, has a shell that measures about 0.6 in (1.5 cm) across. The crab's "happy" markings struck the boy who discovered it as so unusual that he presented it to Japan's Toba Aquarium.

Staff at Japan's Toba Aquarium initially thought this crab's happy face must have been drawn on with a permanent marker.

Full of Heart
In the 1930s, Weaver Blake of Kansas owned a very special horse named Sweetheart. The horse had a heart-shaped birthmark clearly visible on its hide.

Seventh Heaven

There have been many animals that have been born with clear birthmarks of numbers, but none so lucky as those with "7" on their skin. Robert Ripley received dozens of photographs from people who owned calves born with perfect "7s" on their foreheads.

Ready Meal
"Buck" Fulford claimed an astonishing feat by killing, plucking, cooking, and eating a chicken in 1 minute and 50 seconds. His method? He held the chicken upside-down and cut off its head, allowing 40 seconds for it to die, 10 seconds for scalding, 5 seconds to remove feathers, cut out its entrails and cut it into four portions, dropped it into boiling fat for 30 seconds, then placed it in cracked ice for a further 25 seconds!

Take a Pew
The St. Francis Episcopal Church in Stamford, Connecticut, provides special church services, and even Holy Communion, for pets.

Parrot Fashion
A Congo African Gray parrot called N'Kisi, owned by Aimee Morgana of Manhattan, has astonished the scientific world with its vocabulary of more than 700 words. It has also impressed others with its accurate use of tenses of verbs, its keen sense of humor, and even its telepathic abilities.

When it Comes to the Crunch
In a divorce settlement in Edmonton, Canada, Kenneth Duncan was ordered to pay his ex-wife $200 (£105) every month in dog support. On top of that, he also had to dig deep to fund a $2,000 (£1,050) retroactive payment for the care of their St. Bernard, Crunchy.

Silver Service
English eccentric Francis Henry Egerton, the eighth Earl of Bridgewater, had 12 dogs that ate with him every day at formal dinners. The dogs were served from silver dishes.

Married to the Mutt
A nine-year-old Indian girl, Karnamoni Handsa, married a dog in order to ward off an evil omen. Village elders said she would be free to marry a man when she was older, and wouldn't need a divorce from the dog.

Emergency Service
Firefighters in Florida have oxygen masks to help anyone who might have inhaled smoke... including pets. They carry masks for cats, dogs, and even hamsters.

On the Double
This piglet, born in China in 2002, had two heads and three eyes.

Dressed up to the Canines!

The annual ten-day Fantasy Fest held in Key West, Florida, is a chance for everyone to get dressed up and have some fun. It's not just humans who get to join in—pets from across the U.S.A. come to compete in the Pet Masquerade and Parade. Events include the Pet/Owner Look-Alike competition, in which owners and pets dress in matching outfits to suit their chosen theme—ranging from historical figures, such as Marie Antoinette, to sports, such as scuba-diving.

Peri Stone and her pet, Woody, entered in 2002, using The Beatles' "Yellow Submarine" as their theme.

"Miss Trouble," a five-year-old Mexican green iguana entered the Pet/Owner Look-Alike competition in the 2000 Fantasy Fest. Her owner, Todd Heins, took the contest very seriously and did a convincing job of making himself up to resemble his beloved reptile.

Piggy in the Middle

A Bengal tiger called Saimai was suckled by a sow and grew up with a litter of piglets. The unusual family lives peacefully at the Si Racha tiger farm in Thailand.

Pump up the Volume

Serbian farmers have found a secret weapon to help deter the wild boars that destroy their crops: loud rock music. People play it at full volume to scare away their porcine visitors—apparently Meatloaf has proven especially effective.

Unscheduled Departure

Billy the cat was put on to a flight from Phoenix, Arizona, bound for Philadelphia, where he was due to transfer to a connecting international flight. Billy somehow managed to escape from his cage and ended up stuck in the plane's cargo hold for 19 days. Eventually, the cat was discovered at Manchester Airport in New Hampshire, England, and finally reunited with his owners.

Making a Splash

Grey squirrels are renowned for their athleticism, but Twiggy can do more than just climb trees. Under the watchful eye of Florida trainer Lou Ann Best, Twiggy demonstrates her skills as a water-skier at boat shows across America. Twiggy is towed around a 6-in (15-cm) deep inflatable pool at speeds of up to 6 mph (10 km/h) by a remote-controlled model boat. Lou Ann says the key to training Twiggy is affection, patience... and plenty of nuts.

Only the Best

Pigs, cats, monkeys, and even horses are permitted to fly on U.S. airlines—but only in first class.

Finders, Keepers

A Cincinnati couple paid a $10,000 (£5,250) reward to a man who found their dog after it had gone missing.

Animal Hospital

An injured labrador made its own way to Beckley Appalachian Regional Hospital in West Virginia, after it had been hit by a car.

The Downward Dog

A chain of gyms in the U.S.A. offers yoga classes specially designed for dogs and their owners, claiming that the exercise reduces the levels of canine stress.

Litter Bugs

The Feline Evolution CatSeat is a toilet seat for cats, which is mounted on a regular toilet. Apparently it takes two to three weeks for a cat to get used to it.

Going the Whole Hog

Anne Langton of Derbyshire, England, holds the world record for the largest collection of pig-related objects. She owns more than 10,000 porcine knick-knacks, including piggy banks, teapots, kettles, and plush toys.

Speeding Bill

In 2002, a traffic radar camera in northern Germany caught a speeding... duck. The bird must have been flying fast to set off the radar system, but a precise speed could not be determined.

Two Heads are Better than One
Trixie, a blue-tongued lizard with two heads, was discovered in Australia.

Speed Limit
The peregrine falcon is the world's fastest living creature. The birds can reach speeds of between 124 mph (200 km/h) and 168 mph (270 km/h) when swooping from great heights or while catching birds in mid-air.

Cool Mules
Mule Day, a four-day celebration of the humble mule, is held every year in Columbia, Tennessee. Thousands of visitors come from far and wide to attend the festivities, which include mule shows, arts and crafts booths, and a parade.

Paws for Thought
Most cats have five toes on each paw, but Robert Ripley documented many cases of multi-toed cats. One, Whitney, who lived with his owner in New York, had as many as 32 toes—eight on each paw!

Switched On
Monique Cadonic thinks her male cat, Lincoln, a Russian Blue cross, might just be trying to communicate something. Lincoln appears to take great pleasure in batting light switches on and off—particularly when Monique's husband has just got into the shower.

Shaggy Sheep Story
Shrek, a runaway merino ram who was loose for six years in New Zealand, was finally caught by shepherds after surviving several harsh winters. His huge fleece was so overgrown that it weighed 60 lb (27 kg). He was finally shorn by former blade-shearing world champion Peter Casserly—in a speedy 20 minutes! Shrek's fleece was later auctioned for a children's charity.

143

WoRm
His
WaY
OuT

BURIED UP TO his chin in more than 10,000 earthworms, Mark Hogg wormed his way out by actually eating some of them!

Survivalist Mark was gradually buried in the earthworms, then proceeded to eat them—without using his hands—for a whole hour.

That's a whole lot of worms!

Two Ripley employees started to load up the container around Mark.

Keep 'em coming.

Once buried, he was watched by eager spectators as he started to eat.

One of the Family

Maddy, a three-year-old chocolate Labrador retriever, knows just how much her owner loves her because, without the slightest hesitation, he gave her mouth-to-mouth resuscitation. When Maddy got into difficulties in a river, her owner dived in to save her. He then compressed her chest and blew air into her mouth as he performed CPR. He says that's just what you do for family members.

Law and Order

The black squirrels of Council Bluffs, Iowa, are protected by a law that says that people must not "annoy, worry, maim, injure, or kill" any of them.

Slippery Customer

Pulling a snake through your nose and out of your mouth is not everyone's idea of fun, but this man in Madras, India, made a feat of it. He also swallowed 200 worms in 20.22 seconds!

KITTY KAPERS

- 95 per cent of cat-owners admit to talking to their cats
- A cat can jump up to seven times its own height
- A cat can't see directly under its own nose
- A 15-year-old cat has probably spent ten years of its life asleep
- Americans spend more on cat food than on baby food
- The Russian blue cat often has an extra toe
- Cat urine glows under a black light
- Cats have more than 100 vocal sounds; dogs have about ten
- A Texan tabby cat named Dusty gave birth to 420 kittens during her life

Two of a Kind

Scientists in Texas successfully cloned a cat for the first time on December 22, 2001. Rather surprisingly, the aptly named CopyCat owes its existence to a rich dog-lover, Dr. John Sperling, who has poured millions of dollars into research for the Missyplicity Project. The project began as an attempt to clone Sperling's much loved mongrel dog Missy. Sadly, Missy died in 2002, but gene-banking technology means that her DNA is available for cloning when it becomes possible. So far, cloning a cat has proved simpler than cloning a dog, but research continues. As news of the Missyplicity Project spread, requests came in from people all over the world who wanted to clone their own beloved pets. Though it costs many thousands of dollars, cat cloning is now available—and it is thought that dog cloning will be before too long.

A Dog's Life

A seven-year-old boy was raised by a dog in a remote part of Siberia after being abandoned by his parents at the age of three months. When he was found in August 2004 he couldn't talk and had canine traits like walking on all fours, and growling.

In the Dog-house

When Cora the tiger cub was born in a circus in France, her mother didn't have enough milk to feed her. So she was adopted by a kindly pointer called Diane.

I Smell a Cat

The case against a drug suspect in Waterloo, Iowa, was dismissed in 2003 because the police sniffer-dog had failed to complete the search. The highly trained dog had abandoned its duty in order to chase a passing cat.

Doggy Bag

Canadian inventor Paul Le Fevre has come up with a dual-purpose "doggy bag." Although it has a compartment for dog food, it is essentially a designer diaper for dogs so that the streets can be kept clean.

Dandy Warhol

Jacqui Adams is the proud owner of the world's fastest ferret, Warhol. At the 1999 North of England Ferret Racing Championships, Warhol sped 32 ft (10 m) in 12.59 seconds.

Ready, Steady, Slow!

It was a nail-biting finish at the 2004 World Championship Snail Race, as the snails lined up for a life-changing race for fame. The prize-winning mollusk was Owen, who stole the show with a record time, to the delight of his trainer, eight-year-old Joe Clarke from Norfolk, England. Snails secrete mucus from a special gland that enables them to slide on one foot, and they can apparently reach speeds of between 0.029 and 0.0063 mph (0.013 and 0.0028 m/sec).

It took Owen a full 2 minutes, 10 seconds to reach the finish line of the 13-in (33-cm) course.

Asking for Trouble

Trouble, a six-year-old beagle, recently set his paw prints in concrete when he was honored with a place in the Canine World Heroes Walk of Fame. Trouble is a star in the canine world, because he managed to sniff out 1.3 million lb (590,000 kg) of illegal drugs and $27.9 million (£14.6 million) of drug money in 2003.

Bear Necessities

In 2004, a paralyzed Colorado man lay in bed unable to do anything while a 500-lb (227-kg) bear spent two hours ransacking his kitchen for snacks. Known in the area as "Fat Albert," the black bear helped himself to 4 lb (2 kg) of chocolate. Wildlife agents later found Albert sleeping off his sugar high in the man's dining-room.

He'll Have You in Stitches

Baggio, a nine-year-old cockatiel, has stunned his tailor owner, Jack Territo, by learning to sew! The British bird learned his craft by mimicking his owner.

A Feather in her Cap

In 1947, Beverly Bell spent five hours creating this dress made entirely from turkey feathers. It's not just the dress that is made from feathers, the shoes are also made from quill ends.

Ratty and Mole

Moles were causing a real problem in Lincolnshire, England, but when a man decided to hunt for them using his car headlights he wished he hadn't bothered. He crashed the car into his house, the fuel tank exploded, and his home burned to the ground.

Heavy Vetting

Americans spend over six billion dollars per year on vets' fees.

Giving to Swine

Outside a bungalow in Houston, Texas, are signs like "No Porking," and "Pignic Area." A "pigup" truck stands in the driveway and the mailbox is shaped like a pig. The house is Pigdom—owner Victoria Herberta's own hog heaven. Victoria has had a lifelong fascination with pigs, particularly the famous Priscilla, which she taught to swim and sometimes shared a bed with. In 1984, Priscilla rescued a boy from drowning, leading to the creation of a "Priscilla the Pig Day" in Houston in the animal's honor. Although no longer allowed to keep pigs in the city, Victoria's devotion to them endures. "Pigs are intelligent, loving, and sensitive," she says. "I adore them."

Pet Dating

An internet dating agency in the U.K. offers to find companions for dogs—and possibly for their owners as well.

Costume Drama

Dog-owners in Nunoa, Chile, have started a trend of dressing their pets in fancy costumes when taking them for a walk. Dogs about town have been seen dressed as Batman and Robin, Easter bunnies, Cinderella, and Snow White. For more formal occasions, they have even been known to wear tuxedos or wedding dresses!

Steeple Chase

The Dog Chapel, East St. Johnsbury, Vermont, looks like an ordinary white clapboard church— except for the winged dog on the steeple, the stained-glass windows featuring canine characters, and the photographs commemorating dead pets on the walls.

Big Shot

A Michigan man shot at an opossum in his kitchen, but hit a gas line, causing an explosion that caused $45,000 (£23,500) worth of damage.

Frog March

Frog Fantasies is an unusual museum in Eureka Springs, Arkansas. It features nothing but frogs made from porcelain, wood, majolica, jade, coconut, cedar roots, and just about anything else you can think of.

Bundle of Fluff

Crystal is the biggest rabbit in the world, according to her owner, Sue Dooley. The bumper British bunny weighs in at a whopping 27 lb (12 kg).

Groom Service

Luxury pet hotels offer condos and penthouse suites for dogs and cats, complete with ceiling fans and televisions. At PETSuites Pet Resort, pampered pets can also receive grooming and play sessions for an extra charge.

Starling Starlings

No one knows why 300 dead starlings dropped out of the sky in Tacoma, Washington, in 1998. One theory suggests that they were blown to earth by a violent gust of wind.

Lore and Order

Folklore says you can predict the severity of a winter by the coat of the woolly worm, a black and brown caterpillar, in fall. But Jim Morton was confused by their different colors and felt the only way of deciding which worm was right was to hold a race. So each year since 1977, Banner Elk, North Carolina, hosts the Woolly Worm Festival, and the winning worm is the official weather forecaster.

The Lamb and the Unicorn
Both the two-headed lamb and the unicorn were discovered by John Turner of Haddon-on-the-Wall, England.

Ripley's ——®
TWO-HEADED LAMB
EXHIBIT NO: 19546
BORN WITH TWO HEADS ON A FARM
IN ENGLAND

Ripley's ——®
UNICORN LAMB
EXHIBIT NO: 19421
HAD A HORN STICKING OUT OF ITS HEAD,
WHICH MADE IT LOOK LIKE A UNICORN

Coffin Bearer

In a record-breaking stunt, John Lamedica from Delaware lay down in a Plexiglas coffin... with more than 20,000 giant Madagascan hissing cockroaches to keep him company.

Cat Suits

A Japanese website offers tailor-made cat costumes to dress up your pet. Your cat could be a chick, a frog or, strangely, Anne of Green Gables.

It Sticks out a Mile
Phoebe, a Malaysian giant stick insect, is the world's longest bug, measuring a massive 18 in (45 cm).

Croc Climbing

A 13-ft (4-m) crocodile attempted to drag a man from his tent in Queensland, Australia, but was prevented from doing so by a daring 60-year-old woman who jumped on its back. Eventually, someone shot the crocodile. The man and woman both had to be treated for broken bones.

I Smell a Rat

Scientists at the University of Florida have identified neural signals that are transmitted by rats when they locate a scent. This means that eventually the rodents could be used to help in rescue attempts.

MaKe Yourself at Home

BAILEY D. BUFFALO spends more time in his owner's kitchen than in his shed!

Jim and Linda Sautner of Alberta, Canada, raised the buffalo from infancy, hence its tame nature. Bailey weighs 1,650 lb (748 kg), but visits the Sautner house every day.

Bailey D. Buffalo enjoys privileges not usually experienced by buffalo— he's allowed into his owner's kitchen, though he rarely dines with them.

Ten-year-old Carissa Boulden watches her pet horse, Princess, eat a plate of spaghetti at the family's dining table in Sydney, Australia. Princess is even allowed to drink beer on Sundays!

The Lion in Winter
In 2003, Leon the "house lion" kept Radka Sarkanyova and her teddy bear company in the Czech Republic.

The World's Smartest Dog

Chanda-Leah, from Ontario, Canada, is officially the cleverest pooch in the world. She is an 11-year-old poodle that has amassed a repertoire of more than 1,000 tricks, including skateboarding, playing the piano, and untying shoelaces. She and her owner, Sharon Robinson, have performed on TV and toured North America. The performing poodle is also potty trained, and can respond to numerous verbal and hand commands.

Chanda-Leah visits between 150 and 200 hospitals, schools, and nursing homes each year, entertaining everyone with her talented trickery.

Gator Aid

Matthew Goff didn't hesitate to stab a 6-ft (1.8-m) alligator in the eye with his pocket knife after it attempted to nab his puppy, Sugar. When she was off her leash, Sugar wandered to the edge of the pond, and the alligator took the opportunity to grab her head. Fortunately for 29-year-old Matthew, jabbing the reptile in its eye was the right move. Sugar managed to scamper home, with only three teeth marks to show for her near-death experience.

A Meaty Treat

A Moscow company makes meat-based birthday cakes for dogs. They cost about $60 (£30).

Bark 'n Boots

Police in Northumbria, U.K., are issuing their police dogs boots to protect their paws. Police officers think they will prove especially useful in crime scenes where there is glass on the floor.

A Taste of Her Own Medicine

Dr. Perez's patients include people—and their pets. At her practice in Santiago, Chile, she uses alternative medicine to treat conditions such as stress and depression.

The Flying Dachshund

A miniature dachshund called Brutus holds the world record for the highest canine sky-dive: 15,000 ft (4,600 m). Brutus, who lives in California, has made more than 70 sky-dives.

Pup in a Cup

Weighing just 1 lb (450 g) and standing just 4 in (10 cm) tall, Star the Chihuahua stopped growing at just five weeks old. Though she is small, she is still perfectly formed.

PIG HAIR BALL
EXHIBIT NO: 6403
MEASURING MORE THAN 18 IN (46 CM)
IN CIRCUMFERENCE

What a Choker
Pig hair balls are very rough and spikey. Because pigs cannot vomit their hair balls, they can only be found when the animal dies.

Great Balls of Fur
Ripley employee Lisa Shea held the two winning hair balls in the 1994 contest to find the largest hair ball in America. The winning balls were submitted by Mike Cancola of Colorado.

Zebras Crossing
The second Baron Rothschild had a collection of exotic animals at his home in Buckinghamshire, England, in the late 19th century. It included kangaroos, a dingo, giant tortoises, and a team of four zebras that pulled his carriage.

Trunk Call
The Alaska Zoo in Anchorage is building what it believes to be the world's first elephant treadmill. The zoo-keepers need the machine because their 9,120-lb (4,137-kg) elephant, Maggie, is a tad lazy. The final cost of the treadmill could be as much as $250,000 (£130,000).

Neck and Neck
While it is commonly known that the giraffe is the tallest animal in the world, sometimes reaching heights in excess of 18 ft (5.5 m), did you know that it has a tongue that is more than 1 ft (30 cm) long? That means giraffes can lick their own ears!

COW HAIR BALLS
EXHIBIT NO: 6617
THESE WINNING HAIR BALLS ARE 34 IN
(83 CM) IN CIRCUMFERENCE

bad Feather day

Feathered Friend

After terrorizing the residents of Holland, Michigan, for months during 2001, a turkey with a fowl attitude was driven out of town. The aggressive bird had pinned people in their cars or behind their front doors, and menaced any pedestrians who crossed his path.

WHIPPER THE BUDGIE suffers from the bird version of a bad hair day, every day of his life. Born with a rare genetic mutation called "Feather Duster," Whipper was hand-reared by owner Julie Hayward after his parents rejected him.

Not only was he shunned by his own parents—Charles and Camilla—but also by other birds who live in the same New Zealand aviary. The story has a happy ending though, because Whipper now attracts an endless stream of visitors at his new home.

There have only been three cases of the "feather duster" syndrome recorded in the last 60 years.

Loss of Faith

An Oregon man's lost dog was found after an extensive search that lasted two months and involved four psychics and one white witch. The day after the owner got his German shepherd back, the pet-sitter who had been looking after the dog when it went missing, was sued by him for $160,000 (£85,000).

Grin and Bear It

A Romanian shepherd was fleeing from a bear when he slipped and broke his leg. He was rescued by his Pekinese dog, who lured the bear away before returning to its injured owner.

What's Your Poison?

Police were called to an Austrian snake trader's home, but when they got there the man tried to attack them with two poisonous snakes. However, both the cobras bit the snake trader, who then had to be taken to hospital to be injected with an antidote.

Wild Cards

Exotic pets, including two macaque monkeys, a moose, and a raccoon, were seized by police from the home of a millionaire from Alberta, Canada. Apparently, the monkeys, Tarzan and Jane, used to play cards with the family.

Playing Chicken

A British turkey avoided death at Christmas by becoming the surrogate father of some chicken's eggs that were due to hatch.

Mighty Mastiff

Hercules, an English mastiff, who lives with his owner in the U.S.A., weighs a staggering 282 lb (128 kg). The hefty hound entered the record books as the world's largest dog.

Biting Back

A 65-year-old man who was fishing off the coast of Georgia was more than a little shocked when a 30-lb (14-kg) barracuda jumped into his boat and bit him. Apparently, the fish leaped 30 ft (9 m) from the water, as if it had wings, and proceeded to latch on to his finger. The man had to be treated at a hospital for the serious cut.

The Camel's Got the Hump

Jewel, a 1,600-lb (726-kg) aging Bactrian camel at the Brookfield Zoo in Illinois, suffered such arthritis in her front legs that she was nearly lame. However, that's all changed thanks to acupuncture. She's not happy about the needles though, and since camels can kick in any direction, doctors must be nimble during Jewel's treatments.

Drive Time

While his owner watched Canada win the 2004 World Hockey Cup, a dog managed to put a truck into gear and coast down a hill in Whitehorse, Yukon Territory. A man out for a walk alerted police after seeing the vehicle pass with a black Labrador retriever at the wheel.

Rooster Boosters

Organizers of the 2001 New Mexico State Fair Rooster-crowing Contest blamed a quiet event on the heat. Spectators and owners flapped and clucked like chickens in a bid to stimulate activity, but the standard was so low that the winning rooster only had to crow twice.

Bubble Trouble

Connie Beck woke one morning in 2000 to hear strange noises in her home in Howard, Pennsylvania. Upon investigation, she found a deer taking a bubble bath in the bath tub! The deer had not only gained entry to the house, it had also managed to turn on the bathroom tap and knock over the bottle of bubble bath.

Faith Healer

Faith, a Labrador/chow cross, was born without her two front legs and seemed destined to be destroyed. She was saved by Oklahoma City civil servant Jude Stringfellow, and has never looked back. Not only has she mastered the art of walking on two legs like a human being, but she has also become a celebrity—with her own agent, lawyer, and even a part in the latest *Harry Potter* movie.

Hopping Mad

U.S. judge Randy Anglen was reported to be seeking compensation in 2004 after finding a dead mouse in a bottle of beer at his home in Hollister, Missouri. He had drunk the beer by the time he saw the rodent.

Slip into a Nice Bath

German angler Paul Richter doesn't have a rubber duck in his bath—he has been sharing the tub with a giant eel for the past 35 years. When he first caught the slippery creature, his children refused to allow him to cook and eat it. Although his children have now left home, Paul and his wife have become so fond of "Eelfie" that the intended supper has become a family pet that often joins them in the bath.

Can You Dig It?

After being hit by a mail delivery truck, Sweetie the dog showed no signs of life. Distraught owner Glenda Stevens dug a grave and buried her pet in the garden of her home in Park Hills, Missouri. However, hours later she was amazed to see Sweetie's hind legs sticking out of the ground. The dog, which had suffered a broken leg and jaw, was digging itself out of its own grave!

Do You Take This Dog...

After a "love at first sight" meeting while they were being walked by their owners, Saul, a Labrador guide dog, married Foxy, a Border collie in August 2004 at a ceremony organized by Hollywood Hounds. The groom's best man looked on in awe as the bride made her entrance—traditionally late of course—accompanied by bridesmaids Misty, Cara, and Rena. The happy couple's marriage was then blessed by a vicar.

Committed canines Foxy and Saul had 35 guests at their wedding, including the traditional best man and bridesmaids.

On His Last Legs

Boontawee Siengwong, of Bangkok, Thailand, spent 28 days and nights eating and sleeping with 1,000 centipedes in a glass room measuring just 129 sq ft (12 sq m).

Make it Snappy

When Erroberto Piza Rios fancies a game of soccer, he chooses opponents who have a tendency to snap—his pet crocodiles. Erroberto delights tourists on the beach at Iztapa, Mexico, by kicking a ball around with the reptiles, all of which are named after former soccer stars. His favorite trick is to place the ball on one of their heads so that they can lift their powerful jaws and let it roll down their back. He claims never to have been attacked and, in another demonstration, intrigues onlookers by allowing a small crocodile to bite his face gently.

A Day They'll Never Forget

Two pairs of elephants were married in a lavish Valentine's Day ceremony in Ayuthaya, Thailand, in 2001. The elephants wore gowns embroidered with red hearts and even had their trunks brightly painted for the occasion.

The Odd Couple

An orphaned baby hippopotamus has adopted a 100-year-old tortoise as its surrogate mother. The hippo, Owen, which weighs about 650 lb (300 kg), follows the giant tortoise everywhere, and becomes angry and protective whenever the tortoise is approached. They live together at an animal facility in Mombasa, Kenya, Africa.

On All Fours

This cockerel was born in Tirana, Albania, with four legs.

Spiral Island

The 49-year-old English carpenter had thought about building his own island for a long time, and finally took the plunge just south of Cancun in Mexico.

RICHIE SOWA has created his very own tropical island paradise—out of 250,000 plastic water bottles.

The former carpenter from Middlesbrough, England, spent four years constructing

Paper Boat

In March 2003, comedian Tim FitzHigham rowed a paper kayak 160 mi (257 km) down the River Thames to break a 383-year-old record. In 1620, eccentric English poet John Taylor had sailed a paper boat just 40 mi (64 km) down the Thames before his vessel sank. Over eight days Tim rowed from Oxfordshire to London in a boat that was 85 percent paper, the rest being glue to keep out the water. When it did leak, he sealed the holes with sticky tape.

Spiral Island, a raft measuring 66 ft (20 m) by 54 ft (16 m) and floating in a lagoon off the exclusive Mexican resort of Puerto Aventuras. He began with a basic raft made from thick bamboo poles, stuffing the bottles, which he obtained from passers-by, into nets tied to the bottom of the poles. The

air in the bottles helps to keep the island afloat and he has since planted mangroves, the roots of which grow around the bottles to prevent the man-made island from drifting. The real-life Robinson Crusoe has also nailed layers of plywood on to the poles to provide a solid base for his

impressive house, which boasts two bedrooms, a kitchen, and a large living area with walls of plaited palm trees. The roof is covered with plastic sheeting, which collects rainwater for drinking. The mangroves that have been planted help to keep the island cool, and some of them now rise to 15 ft (5 m) high.

Richie Sowa relaxes on the desert island beach that he created just south of Cancun, Mexico, using 250,000 plastic water bottles that were donated by passers-by.

Richie's island home has a large living area, a kitchen, and two bedrooms. The walls are made of plaited palm trees and the roof of plastic sheeting, which also acts as a gutter to collect rainwater for drinking.

Food for Thought

Many prestigious art galleries, including the Museum of Modern Art in New York and the Tate Gallery in London, have purchased works of art made by a group of artists called Mondongo. Their pieces are unusual because of the choice of materials used in making them—cheese, cookies, plasticine, cooked meats, and chopsticks are just a few examples!

Tie Breaker

The world's longest tie—2,300 ft (700 m) long and 82 ft (25 m) wide—has been tied around the Pula Arena, in Croatia. When seagull droppings threatened to ruin the tie, the world's largest owl—a 7-ft (2-m) model—was brought in to guard it.

Chain Reaction

Making a paperclip chain is a serious business for California University student Dan Meyer. Not content with joining half a dozen paperclips, Dan linked 40,000 in one day in February 2004 to form a chain over 1 mi (1.6 km) long!

Coffee Break

The Stella Awards were inspired by Stella Liebeck who, in 1992, spilled a cup of McDonald's coffee onto her lap, burning herself. A New Mexico jury subsequently awarded her $2.9 million (£1.5 million) in damages. Her name is now used as a label for such U.S. lawsuits.

Ringing the Changes

Cinematographer Ed Lachman, who shot the hit movie *Erin Brockovich*, recently tried a new style of filming: using Motorola V710 camera phones. He completed five two-minute videos by using six camera phones set at different angles. He projected the six images together, inspired by the works of cubist artists.

How the Cookie Crumbles

This portrait is made from cookies on wood by the Mondongo group of artists and was exhibited at the Daniel Maman Fine Art Gallery in Buenos Aires in 2004.

The Living Dead

Cary Sharp is known as Honorary Ghost 1,000 in Disneyland's Haunted Mansion after winning Disney's charity auction on eBay in 2004. For his $37,400 (£20,000), the doctor from Baton Rouge, Louisiana, got a personalized tombstone, complete with a humorous epitaph based on his interests and hobbies. Sharp even got to attend his own burial ceremony.

The Veri Thing

The Food and Drug Administration has approved a device called the VeriChip, an implantable computer chip to carry medical files. The size of a grain of rice, it uses radio frequencies to display a patient's blood type and other medical information when activated by a scanner in a doctor's office.

A Cold Snap

Audrey Twitchell of Colorado made her own skiing outfit from 600 Colorado State sales tax tokens, with a combined value of $1.20.

Tiny Guitar

A guitar carved out of crystalline silicon and no bigger than a single cell was made at Cornell University, New York, in 1997. Called the "nanoguitar," it is 10 micrometers long and has six strings, which are inaudible to the human ear. The guitar is so tiny that its shape can only be seen under a microscope.

Playing Away

Joe Cahn, of New Orleans, just hates to miss a single game. Therefore, each fall, for the past nine years, he has hit the road, crisscrossing the United States to attend both NFL and college football games at more than 50 different stadiums. Cahn estimates that by now he must have racked up nearly 300,000 mi (480,000 km) to appease his habit—and in all those miles, he hasn't received a single traffic ticket. The road is never lonely, he says, as he always travels with Sophie, his pet cat.

The Last Straw

Marco Hort in a recent record-breaking attempt managed to fit 210 drinking straws in his mouth!

The Big Picture
Two people were needed to turn one page of this gigantic 16-page book made by Mazda car (manufacturing) company in 2004. It measured 10 ft (3 m) by 11 ft 3 in (3.5 m), and weighed 776 lb (352 kg).

Eco-logical
A Montana couple have built an environmentally friendly house for less than $15,000 (£8,000). Their cozy abode incorporates 13,000 empty soda and beer cans, and 250 used car tires in its foundation. The savings don't stop there: by heating the house with a wood-burning stove and solar power, the couple's utility bills are only $20 (£10) per month.

An Almighty Squash
In 2004, pumpkin-grower Joel Holland produced the winning pumpkin in the 31st annual Safeway World Championship Pumpkin Weigh-off, crushing the chances of 80 other pumpkins to win the prize. Holland had to use a flatbed truck to get his 1,229-lb (557-kg) pumpkin to the competition. To reward his green thumb, Holland received $5 (£2.70) per pound, making his total winnings $6,145 (£3,281).

Can You Believe It?
This replica of the Colosseum in Rome was made using more than 10 million used aluminum cans.

U.S.A.
Montana

It is illegal for married women to go fishing alone on Sundays, and illegal for unmarried women to go fishing alone at all.

No ORdiNaRY TootHpick!

IT'S AMAZING what Michael Drummond of Coco, Florida, can do with a toothpick and a magnifying glass!

More than 30 of Michael's toothpick carvings can be found in various Ripley's museums, including a cowboy complete with horse and lasso, and a butterfly alighting on a flower.

Even a cowboy with a lasso is no match for this miniature carving genius!

Butterflies on flowers are just one of Michael's carving specialities.

Take Your Pick

Bob Shamey of Ligonier, Pennsylvania, creates some of the world's smallest works of art. On an ordinary toothpick, he has carved ornate caricatures of golfers, sailors, fishermen, and aliens. He has even carved a nine-car freight train, and turned a toothpick into a miniature pair of pliers.

Jack O' All Lanterns

In 1982, the "king" of giant pumpkins, Howard Dill of Nova Scotia, Canada, grew the world's largest Jack-o-lantern. It weighed a mighty 445 lb (202 kg) prior to the carving, and measured 10.6 ft (3 m) in circumference.

Catch Your Breath

Shane Shafer, 50, suffered seven months of constant, bark-like hiccups every four seconds before doctors implanted an electronic device in his chest in an innovative operation. All involved breathed long, hiccup-free sighs of relief when Shafer stopped hiccuping.

Watery Grave

A Florida firm offers an unusual resting place for cremated remains: a concrete case on the ocean floor. These "permanent living legacies" are linked to form an artificial commemorative reef in the waters off Palm Beach. Relatives who dive can pay their respects.

Floating Voter

James Pengov, 36, now knows that trying to sell his vote on eBay is illegal. In just 12 hours, authorities heard about—and shut down—Pengov's eBay listing. Pengov, who says he was just trying to pay some medical bills, didn't see the harm in voting for the party favored by his highest bidder, as he was unsure who to vote for.

Take Note

Cops picked up a Pennsylvania resident for passing counterfeit money: a $200 bill (£100) featuring George W. Bush. Clerks at the clothing store didn't know there is no $200 bill. Nor did they notice that it was signed by Ronald Reagan, and that the back showed the White House lawn with signs saying "We Like Broccoli" and "U.S.A. Deserves A Tax Cut."

Steak a Claim

Barcley Prime, an upscale restaurant in Philadelphia, may offer the world's most expensive Philly cheesesteak. Its take on the city favorite, which includes Kobe beef, goose liver, sautéed *foie gras*, caramelized onions, and shaved truffles, costs $100 (£50). By comparison, typical cheesesteaks, which are usually made with thinly sliced ribeye steak and American cheese, run at around $4 (£2).

Banana Republic

More than 6 tons of bananas from the Canary Islands were used in the world's first banana pyramid in Madrid, Spain.

A Knotty Problem
In 1999, Anna Beatrix Zgraggen, from Altdorf, Switzerland, created a tie that was 187 ft (57 m) long, and weighed 400 lb (180 kg). It had to be suspended from a cable car to hang full-length.

Sitting Tenant
After buying a home unseen, a man went to inspect his purchase at Warminster, Pennsylvania—and found a corpse in the living-room. The badly decomposed body was said to be that of the previous owner, a renowned recluse.

Remote Control
Californian inventor Mitch Altman is set to become a hero of TV-haters everywhere. He's the creator of TV-B-Gone™, a key-chain gadget that surreptitiously turns off 1,000 TV models—including those often installed in restaurants, bars, and airports—at the click of a button. Altman was amazed that his initial stocks, which he offered online, sold out in two days.

Fire Starter
A Washington teenager is in such a hot seat that he'll be lucky ever to sit down again; at least in his off-road vehicle. While joyriding—without a condenser—the 18-year-old sparked a forest fire that burned 16,000 acre (6,475 ha). The U.S. Forest Service planned to bill the teenager $10 million (£5 million) to help pay for the costs of fighting the fire, as it is required by law to do so.

Right on Cue
In January 2003, Jack Nemeth, Doug Prenevost, Harlan Ivarson, and Doug Webster played pool continuously for 103 hours in Brooks, Alberta.

Ashes to Ashes
A San Francisco company thinks cremated remains should be displayed in style—and it offers some unique holders. One is an urn made from a liquor cabinet that plays "How Dry I Am" when opened.

Lock, Stock, and Barrel
Vadim Mikhailychev, a teacher from Russia, and his students made a giant lock that weighed 880 lb (400 kg). The key weighed 35 lb (16 kg).

Going Bust

Canadian professional gambler Brian Zembic accepted a $100,000 (£55,000) bet in 1996 that he wouldn't wear female breast implants for a whole year. Not only did he wear the implants and win the bet, but he liked his new 38C breasts so much that he was still showing them off four years later. Brian is no stranger to crazy bets. He previously won a $30,000 (£16,000) wager by spending an entire month in a bathroom.

TOP FIVE WEIRDEST MUSEUMS

1 **Frog Museum** Münchenstein, Switzerland
2 **National Museum of Pasta Foods** Rome, Italy
3 **European Asparagus Museum** Schrobenhausen, Germany
4 **British Lawnmower Museum** Southport, England
5 **Bowling Ball Art Museum** Safety Harbor, Florida

Baby Boom

Michelle Duggar, 37, of Fayetteville, Arkansas, gave birth to her 15th child in May 2004. With the exception of two sets of twins, her children were born one at a time—and all their names begin with "J."

Fast Text

In 2004, British cell phone engineer James Trusler laid claim to being the world's fastest texter. He typed a message requiring 160 taps in just 67 sec live on Australian TV.

Empire Building

The "smallest model of the world's tallest building," this model of the Empire State Building (when it was the world's tallest building), created by Curtis Mathews of Tennessee, took four years to complete. It measured 19.5 ft (6 m) high.

The Smallest Largest

THIS TRAVELING MUSEUM is one of a kind!

The World's Largest Collection of the World's Smallest Versions of the World's Largest Things is a display of miniature replicas of oversized sculptures found across the U.S.A. by founder and curator Erika Nelson. She photographs the many giant objects she passes, and collects information about the sculptures. Then she makes and displays a miniature replica along with the information in her museum!

The World's Smallest Version of the World's Largest Canadian Goose is seen here photographed with its namesake in Sumner, Missouri.

The World's Largest Collection of the World's Smallest Versions of the World's Largest Things museum is situated in none other than a converted Ford Econoline bus!

Domino Effect

A Chinese woman, Ma Lihua, sent the world domino-toppling record crashing in 2003. She took seven weeks to line up 303,628 dominoes (stretching for 9.3 mi or 14 km) and they came tumbling down in just four minutes. The only threat to her record attempt had come from a stray cockroach, which, during the painstaking preparation, had knocked over 10,000 tiles.

Ma Lihua poses for photos with her toppled dominoes after completing her record-breaking feat.

Festive Farewell

Ozella McHargue adored Christmas, so when the native of St. John, Indiana, died in 2004, her family gave her a Christmas-themed funeral. Even though Ozella died in September, her family decorated the funeral parlor with holly, mistletoe, and a Christmas tree, and instead of somber, funereal music, mourners listened to festive classics such as "Rudolph the Red-Nosed Reindeer."

Blowing Hot and Cold

Known as "the fire-proof man," Singlee was a performer at the Ripley Odditorium in Chicago in the 1930s. He is shown here putting a blow torch to his bare skin, including his eyes.

Love and Death

A Canadian couple were married in a funeral chapel in 2001. Shane Neufeld and Christy McKillop chose the unconventional venue in Winnipeg, Manitoba, not only because he worked there, but also because it was where they met.

Body Snatchers

Two desperate thieves stole a hearse from outside a Philadelphia church just as it was waiting to take a corpse to a cemetery. Fortunately the corpse wasn't in the vehicle at the time.

Hide and Go Seek

Author Michael Stadther gives treasure-seekers a challenge in his new book, *A Treasure's Trove*. In it are clues to where he's hidden 12 tokens that can be redeemed for real jewels. It took eight years to find good hiding places in public areas across the United States.

U.S.A.
New Hampshire

You may not tap your feet, nod your head, or in any way keep time to the music in a tavern, restaurant, or cafe.

Dead Man Talking

Mourners at a chapel of rest in Belgium were horrified when a mobile phone rang inside a coffin. The undertaker had forgotten to take it out of the deceased's clothing.

Shark Meat

British property developer Robert Blackwood wants to be fed to Great White sharks when he dies. His bizarre request was inspired by a TV documentary on the sharks.

Jump Ship

Stuntman Robbie Knievel, son of Evel Knievel, jumped seven military aircraft on the deck of an aircraft-carrier in a stunt to promote the launch of a movie about his daredevil father.

Dead Heat

Spiritualist Emma Crawford was buried in 1890 on Red Mountain, near Manitou Springs in Colorado. A landslide in the 1920s suddenly sent her coffin hurtling down into Manitou. Each Halloween the event is commemorated in the Emma Crawford Coffin Races, in which competitors dash along the streets of Manitou carrying coffins containing live Emma look-alikes.

Rainbow Warriors

About 31,000 Filipino students from the Polytechnic University of the Philippines gathered in Manila to form the world's largest human rainbow in 2004.

171

It's Electrifying!

Dr. Dean Ortner used to perform brain surgery on mosquitoes in his former role as a research scientist. Now he's left his lab coat behind to go on the stage, but he still demonstrates his love of science in his "Wonders of Science" programs. His trademark is "riding the lightning," in which he passes a million volts of higher frequency electricity through his body. The power generated makes a board burst into flames, and sends bolts of blue lightning shooting from the fingers of his other hand. He has performed this feat once a week for 30 years, yet he says he's suffered little more than a few burns on his fingertips. The higher frequency doesn't interfere with his nervous system, yet there is still enough power to ignite the wood.

Million Volt Man

Flickers of ionized krypton, xenon, argon, and neon lightning dance around inside a globe, attracted to the touch of Dean Ortner, the Million Volt Man.

Ice and a Slice?
With a room temperature of −5°C (23°F), the Absolut Icebar in Milan, Italy, has to be one of the coolest places to spend an evening!

Pay Your Respects
A man from Schopfheim, Germany, was so keen to save on funeral costs that he tied his dead mother's coffin to his roof rack and drove her along the motorway to the cemetery.

Worm's Eye View

His body wrapped in saran wrap, Welsh performance artist Paul Hurley spent nine days slithering around a field in 2004 to see what life is like as an earthworm. He spent his time burrowing, pausing only to eat a leaf or grain of soil. He saw this as "an exploration of the earth and dirtiness." He has previously coated himself in jelly to become a slug, and dressed as a snail and licked the inside of a greenhouse for two hours.

Off Color
Georgia company Collegiate Memorials allows college football fans to go to their graves proudly displaying their loyalty. The company makes special caskets and urns emblazoned with a university's colors.

Smoke Signal
A Romanian smoker made a coffin out of over 7,000 cigarette packs in 2001. Mihai Cepleuca said he wanted to be buried in it to show that smoking really can put people into their graves.

Turkish Delight
Thousands of Turks helped to carry the world's longest national flag through the center of Istanbul in 2003. At 2.4 mi (3.6 km) long, the flag was created to mark the 80th anniversary of the foundation of the Turkish Republic.

LightNiNG ReacTioNs!

DANIELLE STAMP, otherwise known as Miss Electra, electrified the audience with her dazzling performance for the Ripley's TV show.

As she sat on a giant tesla coil, 2 million volts of electricity were passed through her and out of her fingertips. To top it all, she didn't feel any pain!

Lucky Strike

Being struck by a lightning bolt wasn't that bad at all, according to John Corson, even though the bolt went through his body and then tripped three circuit-breakers in his garage. Since it happened, the 56-year-old says he has been feeling positively energized—he even goes so far as to say he feels ten years younger.

The shocking performance illuminates the audience watching eagerly outside the Ripley's Odditorium in Hollywood, California.

The sparks can be seen flowing through the coil and up into the air, passing through Miss Electra.

Participants hold up two light strobes at which Miss Electra fires bolts from her fingertips!

The Farmer Wants a Wife

An Ohio man paid a farmer to carve the words, "Michelle, will you marry me?" into his corn crop. The bride-to-be melted into giggles—and said "Yes"—when she spied the message from a small plane.

All Hands on Deck
Christina Shaw exhibits a 16 ft (5 m) deckchair sculpture at the Three Counties Show held in Worcestershire, England.

Buried Alive

A 50-year-old Czech man, Zdenek Zahradka, claimed a new world record in June 2004 by surviving for ten days buried underground in a wooden coffin without food or water. He lost 19 lb (9 kg) in weight during his ordeal and said he spent most of his incarceration sleeping.

Balanced Diet

Students from Brigham Young University in, Provo, Utah, balanced 1,290 hand-held eggs simultaneously in 2003. In the course of balancing the eggs, the students broke only half a dozen.

Round the Clock

Jay Larson, founder of the International Speed Golf Association, shot a 72 on a 6,500-yd (5,945-m) course near San Diego, California, in just 39 min 55 sec, averaging less than two-and-a-half minutes per hole. Under the association's rules, the number of strokes is added to the time to calculate the player's score—in Larson's case, 111.55.

Fast Acting

In 1995, Canadian Sean Shannon recited the 260 words of the "To be or not to be" soliloquy from William Shakespeare's *Hamlet* in just 23.8 sec.

No Ordinary Joe

Mastocytosis is an incurable disease that affects approximately one person in every 500,000. Joe Tornatore is one such person: his body experiences anaphylactic shock whenever a foreign substance, such as the venom from a bee sting, enters his body. To protect himself, Joe had to wear a beekeeper's suit, whilst outdoors, for two years. He has written an autobiography all about his experiences while traveling with his suit on, called *Stop and Smell the Silk Roses*.

Joe in his protective suit, posing under a sign he found on his travels, which are documented in his autobiography.

CRAZY GOLF

- American golfer Maud McInnes took 166 strokes on a par-three hole in 1912 after she tried to play the ball out of a river

- Rick Sorensen completed 18 holes at Meadowbrook Golf Club, Minneapolis, in 86 strokes—blindfolded!

- Canada's Moe Norman once teed off in the Los Angeles Open with a Coca-Cola bottle

- In 1914, British golfer J.N. Farrar accepted a bet that he could complete a round in under 100 while carrying full military gear, including rifle and rucksack. He shot a 94

- Australian golfer Rufus Stewart played 18 holes in total darkness in 1931 without losing a ball. He went round in 77

In the Swim

Environmental activist Christopher Swain, of Portland, Oregon, jumps right in if needed. His latest feat was swimming the 80 mi (120 km) of the Charles River, in Massachusetts, to ensure the Environmental Protection Agency keeps to its goal of making it swimmable by 2005. Parts of the river are badly polluted with sewage, trash, and pesticides.

Big Cheese

A South African hypermarket made a 122 ft 8 in (37.4 m) pizza, using 9,920 lb (4,500 kg) of flour, 1,984 lb (900 kg) of tomato puree, 1,984 lb (900 kg) of tomatoes, 3,968 lb (1,800 kg) of cheese, and 1,763 lb (800 kg) of mushrooms. It took 39 hours to prepare and cook.

Holy Smoke!
It took New Yorker, Vincent Pennisi, seven years to create this 38 in (97 cm) high wooden model of Milan Cathedral.

Cookie Monster

A giant chocolate-chip cookie, baked by the Immaculate Baking Company in 2003, weighed in at a staggering 40,000 lb (18,150 kg). Displayed at Flat Rock, North Carolina, it took eight hours to bake, and required 30,000 eggs and a cookie sheet the size of a basketball court!

Have Your Cake and Eat It

In 2004, Serbian baker Zvonko Mihajlovic unveiled what he claimed was the world's biggest birthday cake. Thousands of residents of Nis tucked into the 400-ft (122-m) long cake, which weighed over two tons and used 2,100 eggs and 1,500 lb (680 kg) of sugar.

Bouncing Back

In 1999, David Kirke, of the Dangerous Sports Club, celebrated the 21st anniversary of the first ever bungee jump by repeating the leap off the Clifton Suspension Bridge in Bristol, England.

HiGh FlyiNg!

AS IF WALKING along a beam from one hot-air balloon to another at 4,000 ft (1,220 m) wasn't daring enough, pilot Mike Howard complicated his feat by wearing a blindfold!

The two balloons had been tied together in the skies over Bristol, England, to prevent them from drifting apart. It took Mike a nerve-wracking three minutes to walk the 19-ft (6-m) beam. He then parachuted to the ground to meet his wife and daughter.

Cruise Control
Stuntman David Fish drove a car at 3,500 ft (1,067 m)—strapped to a balloon by steel cables. This wasn't his first hot-air feat. He'd previously had a pillow fight at 5,500 ft (1,676 m), on a bed suspended from a balloon.

Chilling Out

Ian Ashpole relaxed in the comfort of a hammock strung between two hot air balloons, before freefalling and parachuting to the ground.

Armchair Traveler

Balloon pilot Pete Dalby floated above Bristol, England, in the comfort of his armchair, which had been strapped to a specially adapted hot-air balloon.

Madhatters' Tea Party

In 2001, stuntmen Julian Saunders, Rob Oliver, and Ross Taylor became the first people to take tea atop a hot-air balloon. After having tea at 4,920 ft (1,500 m) over Melbourne, Australia, they abseiled down the side of the balloon back into the basket.

Raise a Toast

A half-eaten grilled cheese sandwich sold on eBay for a whopping £15,000 ($28,000). Diana Duyser put the toastie up for sale on the Internet auction site because she was staggered by the likeness of the Virgin Mary that the sandwich bore. The page was viewed more than 100,000 times before the auction ended.

Diana Duyser said she was shocked and scared by the likeness at first, but then put the sandwich up for auction to share the miracle with others.

Pushing the Envelope

When Jeff Datwyler picked up a stray envelope off an Ohio street in 2004, he assumed it was trash. When he opened it, he found a check for $15,000 (£8,000). The irony is that, across town, the person who had lost the envelope was standing in a bank line, blissfully unaware that he'd lost his deposit. Just as he was reaching into his pocket for the envelope, his bank notified him that it had been found.

Short Circuit

The World's Shortest St. Patrick's Day parade took place on March 17, 2004, in the town of Hot Springs, Arkansas. The town staged its parade on Bridge Street, the thoroughfare which, at a quarter the length of a normal city block, has a claim to being the shortest street in the world.

Brought to Book

New York student Steve Stanzak spent seven months sleeping in his university's library because he could not afford accommodation costs. He was finally discovered in April 2004.

A Rise in Inflation

Manoj Chopra of India inflated a hot-water bottle at the World Strongman Cup to display the extraordinary power of his lungs.

BaNaNa GeorGe

GEORGE BLAIR learned to snowboard at 75, drove a racing car for the first time at 81, made his first parachute jump at 82, and took bull-riding lessons at 85!

George is known to everyone as "Banana George" because of his love of all things yellow. He wears yellow clothes, drives a yellow car, and bounces across the lake behind a yellow speedboat.

Age has never been a barrier to the 90-year-old extreme sports fanatic—he made just as much of a splash in 2004, when he was pulled along Florida's Lake Florence at 40 mph (65 km/h), as when he went waterskiing barefoot in icy Antarctica when he was a youthful 71. George's favorite fruit is the banana, and most of his possessions are yellow, even his sunglasses and phone—hence his nickname, "Banana George." In 2002, *Sports Illustrated for Women* put George in the magazine's annual swimsuit issue. "I had never thought of myself as one of the world's sexiest men," he admitted. "But I like it."

George is the world's oldest barefoot waterskier.

He publicizes his favorite fruit so well that he gets sent free bananas.

A Tight Squeeze

In 2003, 14 people from the Kabosh theater group from Belfast, Northern Ireland, squeezed into a phone booth in Edinburgh, Scotland, to break the world record by two people. One said: "It was pretty claustrophobic, but it's a quick way to get to know people!"

U.S.A. Nebraska

In Waterloo, barbers are forbidden from eating onions between 7 a.m. and 7 p.m.

Layer Cake

In 1953, Primo Maca of California baked this 15.6 ft (5 m) tall giant cake, which fed a total of 10,500 people!

Pillow Talk

No fewer than 645 people took part in a mass pillow fight in the town square at Gannet, Kansas, in June 2003.

Heavy Reading

Michael Hawley, a scientist at the Massachusetts Institute of Technology, has written the world's largest published book—a 133-lb (60-kg) tome entitled *Bhutan: A Virtual Odyssey Across the Kingdom*. Measuring 5 ft (1.5 m) by 7 ft (2.1 m), it used 1 gal (4.5 l) of ink and enough paper to cover a football field. The author admitted: "It's not a book to curl up with at bedtime—unless you plan to sleep on it!"

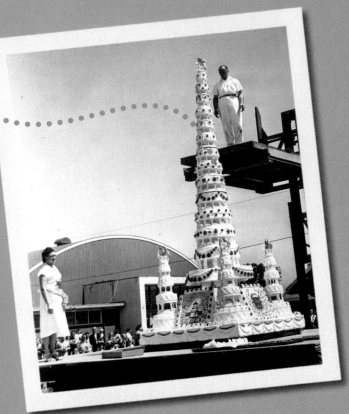

Tip of the Iceberg

Entitled "The Ice Cube Project," this red iceberg floating in Ilulissat Fiord in Greenland, was created in two hours by artist Marco Evaristti, using 6,340 pt (3,000 l) of paint, seawater, three fire hoses, two ice-breakers, and a crew of 20 men.

Pole Star

A former pilot with the Royal Canadian Air Force, Jack Mackenzie joined a nine-member ski expedition to the North Pole in 1999... at the age of 77! To reach the Pole, the sprightly septuagenarian had to ski for up to seven hours a day.

Be Dazzled!

At £15,250 ($29,000), Dazzle is surely the world's most expensive cocktail! A concoction of rosé champagne, strawberry liquor, lychee liquor, lemon juice, and syrup, topped with a white gold and diamond ring, it certainly dazzled diners at the Bar & Brasserie of Harvey Nichols department store in Manchester, England.

The cocktail was part of a "Pink Dinners" month, during which the menu featured an abundance of pink items, from raspberries to pink champagne.

Flower Power

Melvin A. Hember, 82, of St. Charles, Michigan, grew a sunflower in 2001 that had 856 heads and was so heavy that it needed three wooden braces for support. The previous record for a sunflower was a mere 129 heads.

The Pony Express

Indian policeman Sailendra Nath Roy pulled a bus by his ponytail for 100 ft (30 m) in 2003. Previously, he had pulled a van and a jeep with his ponytail and lifted a 45 lb (20 kg) weight with his moustache.

Watt a Bargain

A 40-watt bulb in Fort Worth, Texas, has been burning non-stop for nearly a century! The bulb, which cost just a few cents, was originally fitted above the backstage door at the Palace Theater on September 21, 1908, with orders that it was never to be switched off. Still going strong, it now lights up the Stockyards Museum.

Global Village

In 2001, 13,588 "Village People" danced to the song "YMCA" before a baseball game in Omaha, Nebraska.

Small Talk

Dwarf-tossing contests, such as this one in Surrey, England, are exactly what they sound like. Some say they are offensive, but when the State of Florida banned the pursuit, 3 ft 2 in (96.5 cm) performer Dave Flood sought to overturn the decision so that he could continue to earn a living.

Reaching his Peak

Salvation Mountain near Niland, California, is America's craziest peak. Made from hay bales and adobe, topped with a giant cross, it is 100 ft (30 m) wide and rises three stories high above the desert. Leonard Knight, a former car mechanic who built the mountain 17 years ago, has defied government attempts to demolish it, and lives at its foot in an old truck without electricity or water.

Gift of the Gab

To celebrate the start of her 19th season on U.S. television, talkshow host Oprah Winfrey gave every one of her 276-strong studio audience a brand new $25,000 (£13,000) car.

Man Bites Dog

A 23-year-old man from Bend, Oregon, suspected of assaulting his girlfriend, bit a police dog on the head as he tried to avoid arrest. The dog, named Amor, had just bitten the suspect on the leg.

Baby Bell

Steve Hough is the proud owner of the world's smallest working bell-tower, which he built in his back garden in Gosport, England. Named "Little Ben" it's a tribute to its larger namesake, London's Big Ben.

Pushing His Luck

A man was arrested in Blue Lake, California, in 2004 after police officers saw him doing one-handed push-ups in the middle of the State Highway 299. He was trying to get a lift home and thought his daring fitness routine would force a driver to stop for him!

Wind Bag

Solicitor's clerk Paul Hunn from London, England, trains on an unusual diet of carbonated drinks and spicy foods. Why? He is the world's loudest burper! In 2000, Paul belched at 118.1 decibels—as loud as a pneumatic drill.

Butter Nuts

A Swedish couple out hunting in the northern province of Jaemtland were alarmed to stumble across 70 pairs of shoes, all filled with butter. Sneakers, stilettos, and boots were all stuffed with 1 lb (0.5 kg) of butter and spread out over the landscape.

Binocular Vision
Frank Gehry designed this spectacular binocular-shaped building in Venice, Los Angeles.

Super Sculptures!

THE U.S.A. IS HOME to a spectacular range of oversized sculptures.

Minnesota is littered with such attractions, and one of them is a 33-ft (10-m) tall statue of the legendary lumberjack Paul Bunyan, in front of the Paul Bunyan Historical Society Museum in Akeley.

High Point, North Carolina, the self-proclaimed "Home Furnishing Capital of the World" boasts a 33-ft (10-m) chest of drawers. The attraction has stood there since the Chamber of Commerce built it in 1926.

The 12-ft (4-m) prairie dog statue in Interior, South Dakota, stands guard outside The Ranch Store souvenir stand. Not only can you see the world's largest prairie dog statue here, but you can also feed or even buy real prairie dogs.

Hair Pin

Who would have thought that it's possible to drill holes through a human hair? J.M. Thompson of Philadelphia did—each hole, shown below, measured 0.0007 in (0.002 cm)! Howard Adam of Wisconsin even managed to thread a human hair through a drilled hair.

Riding High

Life is one long rollercoaster ride for Chicago university lecturer Richard Rodriguez. He has been setting rollercoaster endurance records since the 1970s, and in 2003 at an amusement park in Berlin, Germany, he set a new mark of 195 hours. He used two trains for the attempt, one car on each being equipped with a small toilet, as well as cushions for him to sleep on.

The Sound of Silence

In February 2003, musicians in Halberstadt, Germany, played the first three notes of what will be by far the world's longest concert. They have stretched a 20-minute piano piece by avant-garde American composer John Cage to last... 639 years. The concert actually started in September 2001, but as Cage's piece began with a rest, there were 18 months of silence leading into the opening notes.

Toilet Humor

Unusual flying machines were the theme for the 2003 coastal flying demonstrations in France. Approximately 8,000 pilots gathered to exhibit their wacky flyers, such as this slipper-happy paraglider.

Licence to Thrill

Fred Hale Sr. of New York got his driving licence in 1995—at age 104. He carried on driving until it expired on his 108th birthday.

The Smallest Show on Earth

Spending £1,000 ($1,900) installing soundproofing, a projection booth, and velvet seats from his local Odeon theater, Englishman David Alligan has converted his garden shed into a cinema with an 8-ft (2.5-m) screen.

Cool Customer

In January 2003, Jin Songhao broke his own record by standing naked in freezing conditions for four hours. The 48-year-old stood in a quiet spot near Harbin, China, in temperatures that plunged to −29°C (−20°F).

Melting Point

A 2004 attempt to break the world record for the longest hockey game was abandoned after a full 87 hours and 10 minutes of play because the ice in Edmonton, Alberta, began to melt—due to unseasonably high temperatures. The players were trying to break the existing record of 130 hours and 7 minutes set by the Moosomin, Saskatchewan, Moose Fraternity in 2003.

Get the Message?

Mexican Laura Carmona made her message loud and clear to boyfriend Alfonso Hernandez when she covered his car in love letters on St. Valentine's Day!

Taking the Plunge

A Canadian prankster plunged into the pool during the men's diving competition at the 2004 Athens Olympics wearing a tutu and tights!

Dead Ringers

The funeral of Dane Squires was interrupted in 2004 when the deceased phoned his family to say he wasn't dead! His sister had identified him as the victim of a railroad accident in Toronto, Ontario, but the burial was put on hold when Dane called to say that the mutilated body was someone else's.

Leap of Faith

Fitted with artificial knees and a hearing-aid, 92-year-old Herb Tanner completed his first parachute jump in 1998 when he leaped from a plane 3,500 ft (1,067 m) above Cleveland, Ohio. A pilot for 63 years, Herb had always wanted to make a parachute jump, but his wife had threatened to leave him if he ever did so. When she died in 1996, he was finally able to make his dream come true.

Stamp of Approval

The German Post Office in Berlin promoted their building by covering all 130,000 sq ft (12,000 sq m) of it with thousands of love letters.

CoiNinG It!

The mid-1980s MGB Roadster, which is covered in gold-plated English pennies, is currently on display at the Ripley's Museum in Mexico.

YOU COULD SAY that Ken Burkitt of Niagara Falls, Ontario, Canada, is money mad!

Ken's obsession with coins is not confined to his wallet—he has decorated several cars with coins and he spends his time making sure he covers every inch of them. Ken covered this

Mini and a limousine with thousands of them. All of the cars Ken has decorated are in full working order—in fact, they are in mint condition! Each coin that Ken uses is covered with at least eight coats of polyurethane, in order to stop them from discoloring or rusting.

Gold-plated English pennies cover this 1988 Lincoln Continental stretch limousine, part of the Ripley collection.

On most of the cars he decorates, Ken uses coins of various vintages, dating back to the 1860s.

Annie Burkitt

Ken is not the only creative one in the family. His wife, Annie Burkitt, creates portraits of famous people, such as John Lennon, Marilyn Monroe, and Louis Armstrong, from cut lead crystals.

Coins are bent into shape using a vice to make the coins cover every inch of the car.

Ripley's®
COIN-COVERED MINI
EXHIBIT NO: 11647
1969 AUSTIN MINI COVERED IN
GOLD-PLATED ENGLISH PENNIES

Way to Mow!

Gary Hatter of Champaign, Illinois, made a 14,500-mi (22,000-km) journey around America—on a lawnmower! Leaving Portland, Maine, in May 2000, he passed through all 48 continuous U.S. states and dipped into Canada and Mexico, before arriving at Daytona Beach, Florida, in February 2001. One of his proudest moments came halfway through the 260 days of riding when, in Iowa, he overtook another vehicle!

Pole Position

Jenefer Davies Mansfield, a choreographer, staged her *NASCAR Ballet* at a Virginia theater in 2003. The production featured 20 dancers clad in corporate patches of the theater's sponsors. As they leapt around a banked-racetrack stage, occasionally crashing into each other, the dancers were accompanied by the sounds of revving engines. Mansfield hoped to entice NASCAR fans who were in the area for race day.

Tall Order

In 1989, Randall Jones of Georgia built what is believed to be the world's tallest bicycle. It stands at 17 ft 2 in (5 m) tall. The diameter of the front wheel is 26 ft (8 m).

U.S.A.
California

In Blythe, you are not permitted to wear cowboy boots unless you already own at least two cows.

The Car's the Star

Some of the strangest looking vehicles in America can be found at the Art Car Museum in Houston, Texas. Eccentric owners have decorated their cars to reflect their personalities, covering them in everything from buttons and pennies, to grass and flowers. Among the most colorful exhibits are the Roachster, a vehicle decorated like a cockroach; the Swamp Mutha, adorned with birds and curious creatures; Faith, which has a buffalo head at the front of the car; and Rex Rabbit, a car designed in the shape of a huge rabbit.

You Shall Go to the Ball!

Originally a boat that was used to sail the canals of Venice, this wooden Cinderella's carriage has been converted into a roadworthy vehicle—it's even been used as a wedding carriage.

Boy Racer

Robb Lapeen from Flint, Michigan, jumped over nine cars on his motorbike—when he was just eight years old. He has been riding motorbikes since he was two and first raced on ice and dirt at the age of four.

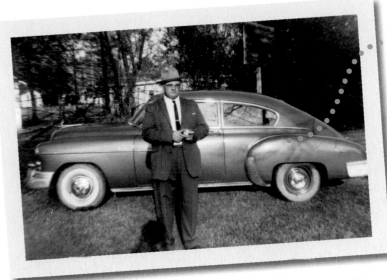

• You Win Some...
Dennis L. Wheat, from Malvern, Arkansas, won his car in a raffle. Unlucky for him, however, he later discovered that it was the same car he had traded-in six years earlier!

Crash Test Dummy

A Toronto teenager crashed into six cars as she completed the parking maneuver of her 2001 driving test. She was all set to pass until she turned into the parking lot of the test center, and accidentally pressed the accelerator, hitting the cars.

Emergency Exit

When 41-year-old Fidel Cueva decided to exit a Greyhound bus window, it didn't seem to matter to him that the bus was traveling at 55 mph (90 km/h) through rush-hour traffic. Perhaps it was because he was so upset that the express bus had just bypassed his stop.

Supply and Demand

Hyperactive Technologies, a company based in Pittsburgh, currently offers software to fast-food restaurants that predicts customer rushes. The "Hyperactive Bob" system predicts demand using rooftop cameras that monitor traffic entering the eateries' parking lots and drive-thru lanes. By the end of 2005, however, restaurant managers should be able to access software that predicts what customers will actually order—based on the vehicle that they drive.

Sailing in the Cart

In December 2003, the intrepid Mark McGowan announced that he was planning to sail from London to Glasgow—in a supermarket shopping cart! Attaching a sail to the cart to make use of northerly winds, and with a broom for propulsion and steering, he set off on the maiden voyage of *Ocean Wave II*, hoping to complete the 400-mi (600-km) journey in around nine months. He planned to sing Rod Stewart's "Sailing" every day to keep up his spirits. Alas, after just 65 mi (100 km) he abandoned the voyage because of icy conditions. Undeterred, he embarked on a fresh challenge and pulled a television set through the streets of Milan for 4 mi (6 km)—using a rope tied to his ear.

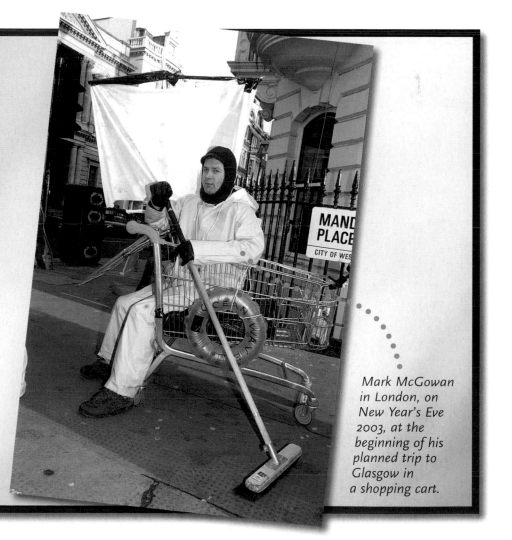

Mark McGowan in London, on New Year's Eve 2003, at the beginning of his planned trip to Glasgow in a shopping cart.

End of the Line

In 2001, over 400 New York subway cars were pushed into the sea by a bulldozer off Cape Hanlopen, Delaware. They landed 80 ft (25 m) under the surface of the Atlantic. The aim was to create an artificial reef, attracting more fish.

On the Rocks

The Princess May, which ran aground in 1910 on Sentinel Island, Alaska, during a low tide rose 30 ft (9 m) in the air! Tugs eventually pulled the vessel from the rocks.

The Bicycle Thief

Ken James of Melbourne, Australia, died when he fell off a bicycle he had stolen. Police found more than 400 stolen bikes at his home.

How Low Can You Go?

Andy Saunders has customized his 1985 Mini in a unique way—by making it the lowest in the world. The mini Mini is just 34 in (86 cm) high.

Full of Hot-Air

This monster truck was created by Scottish balloon artist Colin Myles in 2003. Colin has made all sorts of sculptures from balloons, such as a liquorice man, a giant sunflower, and animals including bears and kangaroos.

Rock Lobster
The Art Car Weekend, held annually in Houston, Texas, attracts a host of unusual vehicles, including this cute crustacean.

Wheely Slow
A 73-year-old Milwaukee man irked motorists by traveling on the highway at 5 mph (8 km/h)—in his wheelchair. Despite the fact that wheelchairs aren't allowed on the highway, the man took his chances after a transportation service failed to pick him up for his doctor's appointment.

Starting Young
In 2003, after the keys had been left in the ignition of Taccara King's pickup, her two-year-old son started it and crashed it into a transport office at Vero Beach, Florida.

Pedal Power
Grand Prix rules apply in an annual pedal-powered car race. Competitors race around streets in Valentigney, France, with drivers and cars in costume: recent races have seen banana cars with monkey drivers and pumpkin cars with witches at the wheel. The winner is judged on the basis of both speed and costume.

Put Your Foot on the Gas
Roman Kunikov, a Russian professor, has designed gasoline-powered boots. Tests in a public square at Ufa, near Moscow, showed that wearers could achieve speeds of up to 25 mph (40 km/h).

Baling Out
In 2003, in Makoti, North Dakota, John Smith, also known as the "Flying Farmer," jumped his car over 25 bales of hay—covering a total distance of 160 ft (50 m). John had told his wife earlier that year that if he hadn't sold the hay bales by the start of February, he would jump over them in his car.

ON THE MOVE
- Until 1979, the Egyptian driving test consisted of driving 20 ft (6 m) forward and then the same in reverse
- An English woman took 330 driving lessons and 48 tests before finally passing in 1987
- Instead of windscreen wipers, drivers of the first cars rubbed potatoes over the glass to help the rainwater run off
- Helen Ireland of Auburn, California, failed her driving test when she drove straight into the wall of the test center

A Barrel of Laughs
Speeds of up to 15 mph (20 km/h) can be reached by these wacky racers of beer kegs, in Windsor, England.

High-flyer

Setting the world record for the highest human flight with a rocket belt, American stunt expert Eric Scott reached a height of 152 ft (46 m). He strapped the rocket belt around his waist and, with the aid of the jetpack on his back, took off in the skies over London in 2004.

U.S.A.
Indiana

In Gary, a person may not enter a movie house, theater, or ride a public streetcar within four hours of eating garlic.

Sticky Situation

A West Virginia woman was literally glued to the floor, when she didn't realize that the 3M liquid bandage she had applied to her heel had dripped down to her toes. Family members had to call 911, and three paramedics took more than an hour and a bottle of baby oil to free her. The woman said the humiliation of still being in her robe was by far the worst part of the experience.

Hamburger Harley

Harry Sperl rides around Daytona Beach, Florida, with relish—on an 1100cc Harley-Davidson trike that has been covered with a huge Fiberglass-and-Styrofoam hamburger. The Hamburger Harley comes with a melting-cheese fender and ketchup-bottle shock covers. Harry's love for bikes is matched only by his passion for burgers. He also owns the world's only Hamburger Museum.

Rocket Man

By fitting 24 rockets to his luge, a light toboggan, Billy Copeland of Ashland City, Tennessee, can reach speeds of nearly 100 mph (160 km/h) in just six seconds on steep hills.

Higher Car

Gary Duval of Colton, California, has built a car that measures 10 ft 11 in (4 m) high from the ground to the roof. It sits on eight monster truck tires, has two separate engines, and took more than 4,000 hours to build.

Tug of Love

In 2000, 20 men pulled an 18-ton dump truck around a parking lot in Kenosha, Wisconsin... for an hour without stopping. By the end, they had pulled the truck a total distance of 3.3 mi (5 km).

Talking Turkey

Josh Harper overslept on Christmas Day 2002 and had to drive to his girlfriend's house for dinner, so he decided to cook the turkey on his car engine while he traveled the 90 mi (135 km) to her home in Bristol, England. "The potatoes were a little firm," he said, "but the turkey was done to a treat."

Toilet Roll

In 1999, Hank Harp drove a motorized toilet the length of Britain—a total of 874 mi (1,300 km). He sat on the seat of the chemical toilet, which was powered by an electric motor and had a top speed of 4 mph (6 km/h), and stored the supplies that he needed for his journey in the bowl.

On his Knees
Australian charity worker Suresh Joachim attempted to break the world record for a continuous crawl in 2001. The current record, which was set in 1992, stands at 31.4 mi (50.6 km): to break this, Joachim needed to complete 2,500 laps of his enclosure on the streets of Sydney, Australia.

Milking it

Sam Draper and Julie Magenis of Houston, Texas, have turned a 1979 Cadillac into the Cow-de-lac. Painted black and white like a Friesian cow, the car has an Astroturf interior and upholstery made from feed and potato sacks. The hood is adorned with model cows while the roof displays a farmyard scene.

Revving up

English vicar Rev. Paul Sinclair, also known as the "Faster Pastor," has a sidecar hearse on his motorcycle so that he can give deceased bikers a suitable send-off. It cost £30,000 ($58,000) to convert his 955cc machine, which can hold a coffin at speeds of up to 70 mph (115 km/h).

Jump to it

Texan parachutist Mike Zang managed to jump out of a plane 500 times in less than 24 hours over Fort Worth, Texas, in May 2001. This means he achieved an average of one parachute jump every three minutes, despite mechanical problems, lightning, and heavy rain.

Ripley's®

STICK ROLLS ROYCE
EXHIBIT NO: 13081
TOOK 4,609 HOURS TO COMPLETE, AND MEASURES 12 FT 8 IN (4 M) IN LENGTH

Match That
More than 1 million matchsticks went into the construction of this Rolls-Royce, made by Englishman Reg Pollard in 1987. He used the most matchsticks ever recorded in one model—1,016,711!

Pulling Power

In 1990, bodybuilder Georges Christen decided to test his pulling power by holding on to ropes attached to three light aircraft as they attempted to take off.

Not in my Backyard

Back in 1969, when he was still studying at high school, Kim Pedersen made the initial sketches of a monorail he wanted to build in his backyard. Unsurprisingly, his parents dismissed the whole idea, but now that Kim has a place of his own, he has finally been able to realize his dream. Consequently, his home in Fremont, California, is probably the only one in the world with a working monorail in the backyard. The track runs 300 ft (90 m) around the perimeter of his backyard and is 8 ft (2.4 m) tall at its highest point. The monorail took five years to construct, at a cost of $4,000 (£2,000), but monorail-mad Kim reckons it's worth every cent!

The Fastest Milkman in the West

Welsh racing-driver Richard Rozhon established the inaugural world speed record for the electric milk-float. He managed to get the humble machine to accumulate 73 mph (117 km/h) at a milk-float speed trial in Leicestershire, England, in 2003.

Way to Go

The Appian Way, which originally connected Rome, Italy, with Capua, was so well built that it is still in use after more than 2,000 years. The 4-ft (1-m) thick highway, which is more than 350 mi (525 km) long, would cost more than $500,000 (£260,000) a mile to build today.

The Jet Set

The latest pastime for thrill-seeking adrenalin junkies on the Caribbean island of St. Marten is to stand on the beach at the end of the runway at Princess Juliana International Airport and try to remain upright as the huge airplanes take off. People have been tossed in the air by the sheer force of the planes flying so low overhead.

First-class Lounge

As a nine-year-old boy, Gregory Langley always flew first-class—because he had a seat from his favorite plane, Concorde, installed in his home.

DestiNed for GREAT Heights

AT TEN YEARS old Paul Hill could have been the world's youngest pilot, and he was certainly the youngest boy in England ever to fly a plane.

Paul's dream to fly Concorde may not have come true, but he was delighted with his successful take-offs and landings.

Paul successfully flew a Cessna 150—with a qualified co-pilot.

After watching his father, Terry, take flying lessons, Paul soon picked up the necessary skills, although he couldn't fly solo until he turned 17.

Making a Splash
In 1998, Frenchman Alain Vagh created a ceramic-tiled bath to his own specifications—nothing unusual about that, except that it was installed in the back of his Jeep! Now his kids can splash about as much as they like while bathing on the open road.

Tanks Very Much
An Austrian soldier was fined for speeding... in a 25-ton tank. Even though he was on a military exercise, the soldier had to pay the fine for driving at 40 mph (60 km/h) within a 30 mph (50 km/h) zone.

Blind Faith
Scott Duncan and Pamela Habek set off from their home city of San Francisco in October 2004 in a bid to sail around the world alone—even though they are both legally blind. They are relying on electronic aids to navigate their 32-ft (10-m) cutter, Tournesol, on a unique voyage that is expected to take two years.

Starring Rolls
Graham Crossley of Sheffield, England, is crazy about Rolls-Royces—even though he can't drive. The 41-year-old has been in love with Rollers since the age of 11. He has a collection of more than 2,500 photographs, tours garages, and often spends his weekends washing other people's Rolls-Royces for nothing—just so that he can get close to his favorite cars.

Take the Long Way Home
A luxury limousine that contains a king-sized waterbed—and even a swimming pool—holds the record as the longest car ever built. The 1980 Cadillac stretches to 100 ft (30 m) long and has 26 wheels.

Sign of the Times
Confused by a Los Angeles freeway sign, artist Richard Ankrom took matters into his own hands in 2001. He scaled the sign and added a vital direction so well that state officials were unable to detect the alteration. After tracking down the authentic reflective buttons that make up each letter from a company in Tacoma, Washington, he added the helpful word "north" to the sign. While making the change, he wore a hard hat and orange fluorescent vest to avert suspicion.

Beer Necessities

Police in Grand Island, Nebraska reported that after a heavy snowstorm in 2001, a man stole a snowplow from Hastings storage shed and drove it 20 mi (30 km)—just to buy a case of beer.

Going Flat Out

In 1995, Dutch cyclist Fred Rompelberg achieved the highest ever recorded speed on a bicycle—more than 167 mph (269 km/h)—at Bonneville Salt Flats, Utah.

Space Race

The crew of the command module *Apollo 10* became the fastest human beings ever when the module reached 24,791 mph (39,900 km/h).

Self-Build

Measuring 19 ft 4 in (6 m) in length and weighing 2,800 lb (1,270 kg), this Longhorn V-12 took Texan Oliver Albert 12 years to build—by hand! Oliver built it using the best parts of more than 14 different types of vehicle—including a Cadillac, Chevrolet, Chrysler, Dodge, Ford, Jeep, Lincoln, Mercedes, Mercury, Nash, Plymouth, Pontiac, Renault, and Terraplane.

Breaking Step

The San Francisco Bay to Breakers foot race attracts up to 75,000 runners, many of them in a variety of costumes such as giant chickens, Batman, and sets of dominoes.

In the Name of the Lawn

The National Lawnmower Racing Championships take place in Mendota, Illinois. The race started out as an April Fools' joke in 1992, but has proved so popular that it has become an annual event.

Head Over Heels

This giant stiletto was built in the Philippines around a 1,000 cc Japanese motorbike.

Keeping his Cool

In February 2000, actor Paul Newman became the world's oldest racing driver when he competed at the Daytona International Speedway in Florida. He was 75 years and 11 days old on the day—and his co-driver was just 17.

FLIGHT PLAN

- At any time of day, more than 60,000 people are airborne over the U.S.A.
- The wingspan of a Boeing 747 is longer than the Wright brothers' maiden flight
- Chicago's O'Hare International Airport is the world's busiest. An airplane takes off or lands every 37 seconds
- The first female flight attendants were required to weigh no more than 115 lb (52 kg), to be trained nurses, and to be unmarried!

You Wanna Jet?
Andy Green reached an amazing 763.03 mph (1,227.98 km/h) in *Thrust*, his twin-jet-engine, supersonic car, in October 1997. He established a world land-speed record at the event in the Black Rock Desert, Nevada.

Another Fine Mess
A massive speeding fine of more than $200,000 (£105,000) was issued to millionaire Jussi Salonoja in Finland in 2004. The amount was calculated to reflect Mr. Salonoja's large income.

• From the Bottom to ZZ Top
Depicting many world-famous musicians—including ZZ Top, Madonna, Jimi Hendrix, and Sir Elton John—the creators intended to purvey the message "music lives forever." The car is decorated with sculpted styrofoam, and covered with beads, glass, jewelry, and albums.

Ripley's®
"GRATEFUL UNDEAD" EXHIBIT NO: 21480
CREATED BY HOUSTON ART TEACHER
REBECCA BASS AND 19 ART STUDENTS

Reach for the Skies
The annual run up the Empire State Building has imitators all over the world, including a run up the monumental Petronas Towers in Malaysia.

Table Mountain
The Annual Furniture Race in Whitefish, Montana, involves competitors attaching skis to various items of furniture and racing down the nearby Big Mountain.

Pump up the Volume

A never-to-be-forgotten family reunion of 55 members—aged from three to 37—was organized by Roger Dumas. Dumas labored for more than 20 years to build a bicycle that could hold them all! During the construction process, he used parts from 150 other bicycles, but Dumas claimed that the vehicle was built entirely without plans.

It's a Knockout

In November 2004, Romanian Alin Popescu stole a car and then crashed into a tree and knocked himself out after traveling half a mile. He was lucky not to have been killed, especially since he is blind.

Going on a Bender

Uri Geller became famous as a spoon-bending psychic. His art car, called "The Geller Effect," is a Cadillac completely covered with thousands of pieces of bent cutlery.

Galloping Gormets

The 26-mi (40-km) course of *Le Marathon du Cahors et de la Gastronomie* in France is dotted with feeding stations serving foie gras paté, truffles, and copious quantities of wine. Most competitors are in fancy dress, and the race is followed by a wine festival.

Canada

In Alberta, if you are released from prison, it is required that you are given a handgun with bullets and a horse, so you can ride out of town.

One Careful Owner

Retired science teacher Irvin Gordon of East Patchogue, New York, drives a 1966 Volvo P1800S that has well over 2 million mi (3 million km) on the clock—the highest mileage recorded by any car in the world. Irvin has been the car's only owner—he bought it new in June 1966. He used to commute 125 mi (200 km) to work every day, and loves his car so much that since he retired he often drives to other states for lunch.

Engine Room

Two production cars that were built in the early 20th century hold the record for the largest engine capacity. The Peerless 6-60, which was built between 1912 and 1914, and the Fageol, which was built in 1918, both had 13.5-liter engines.

Dead Heat

Manitou Springs, Colorado, is famous for its annual coffin races, in which competitors zoom down the town's main street in wheeled coffins.

Recycled Cycles

In the 1930s, Joseph Steinlauf, a mechanic from Chicago, Illinois, created bicycles made from all sorts of material, including guns, a sewing machine, and even an old headboard and a hot-water bottle! The gun bicycle weighed about 350 lb (160 kg).

Wheel of FiRe

KNOWN AS "PYRO BOY," website-designer Wally Glenn's life is a hotbed of flames!

Wally Glenn walks through rings of flames, wearing a fire-retardant suit, and with explosives strapped to his body. At a death-defying event at Ripley's Aquarium in Myrtle Beach, South Carolina, in November 1999, Pyro Boy braved temperatures as high as 2,000 °F (1,100 °C).

Pyro Boy designed his own helmet and outfit, which were made from fire-retardant material.

Once inside the suit, 20 lb (9 kg) of explosives were strapped to his body.

Pyro Boy bravely walks through rings of fire. Once he was unharmed, but another time he caught fire!

The event was more than just a flash in the pan: it was recorded for the Ripley television show in November 1999 at Ripley's Aquarium in Myrtle Beach, South Carolina.

With temperatures reaching as high as 2,000 F° (1,100 C°) outside the suit, it's no surprise that Pyro Boy's neck was singed beneath his suit.

He Sure Can Carry a Note
J. Clark Cullom, of Cincinnati, Ohio, carried a piano with him wherever he went! He traveled more than 15,000 mi (23,000 km) with it strapped to his car.

Hitting the Roof
A Massachusetts man was getting ready for his Fourth of July cookout when the fireworks started early: a Ford Taurus drove off an elevated parking lot and crashed through the roof of his house. No one was hurt in the freak accident, but guests were surprised to see the car sticking out of the roof when they arrived to begin the celebrations.

Good Day at the Office, Dear?
Swapping desks was taken to new extremes when Edd China invented the world's first "office car." The road-worthy workspace made its debut in London, England, in 2003, at the start of a 900-mi (1,500-km) charity road trip to the South of France.

Boom or Bust
Dannie Eaves, an employee at an Oregon bronze shop, was pulled over by police because of six busts in his pickup truck. Dismayed motorists mistook the sculptures for dead bodies and called the cops.

A Dream Wedding
A bride's dream of a memorable wedding came true when she arrived at the ceremony in a four-poster bed on wheels. Lisa Turner followed groom Simon Croft, who traveled in a mobile office, complete with boardroom table and water cooler, in a bizarre 5-mi (8-km) procession in Hampshire, England, in 2004.

DRIVE DOWN YOUR 'TOTAL' OFFICE COSTS
with beoffices.com

H116 HDY

Bouncing Babies

In a freak accident, two young toddlers fell three stories from a Los Angeles apartment window—and lived. The resilient toddlers were taken to the hospital to be checked out, but soon recovered.

Dead Man Walking

Despite the fact that his family thought he'd been hit by a train, Dane Squires of Toronto was very much alive—and in the dark about arrangements for his funeral service. He called his daughter's cell phone just as his casket was being loaded into a hearse, causing her to freak out, believing his ghost was trying to contact her. The man's sister had previously identified the dead body to be his.

Blind Ambition

Being blind hasn't stopped Mike Newman setting speed records. He set the first world record for unsighted driving on a motorbike at 89 mph (143 km/h) in 2001. Then, in 2003, he broke the record for unsighted driving when he reached 144 mph (232 km/h) in a Jaguar XJR.

All Aboard!

All 34 members of India's Army Services Corps Tornadoes go for a spin on an Indian-built Enfield Bullet 500cc motorcycle in Bangalore in June 2004.

Wheels on Fire

Roller-blading was no easy task back in 1906. Inventor Alphonse Constantitni invented motor-driven skates—they could travel at up to 40 mph (64 km/h).

Wind Tunnel

Slow riders in the Netherlands needn't worry—there is an 8-mi (13-km) long tunnel that contains massive electric fans—they push along riders at up to 28 mph (45 km/h).

Bag of Tricks

Indian magician O.P. Sharma drives a motorbike as part of a stunt, with a black bag over his head in August 2004—and it wasn't on an empty road, but a busy street in the city of Patna.

A Fishy Business

If you ask Singapore businessman Lawrence Ng what's in the tank of his Jaguar, the answer is simple: fish. By ripping out the seats and engine, and sealing the windows and doors, he has converted his car into a big fish tank. The trunk and hood are home to filter systems and air pumps, and the fish are fed through the sunroof.

New York Minute

It has been calculated that people in New York travel, on average, a farther distance vertically than they do horizontally. This is due to the height of the many tall buildings, which makes it necessary to climb more than walk on the level.

Wheely Fast

The fastest speed ever achieved on a motorcycle is 322 mph (518 km/h). Dave Campos set the record at Bonneville Salt Flats, Utah, in 1990.

Crash Course

A truck driver deliberately crashed his truck into a parked car outside a bank in Olhsdorf, Austria, thinking it was a getaway vehicle. It wasn't, and the truck driver was liable for repairs and a hefty fine.

The Sky's the Limit

The new Airbus A380 will be the world's largest aircraft when it comes into service in 2007. Its wingspan is nearly 262 ft (80 m), and it stands 80 ft (25 m) tall. The plane will be fitted with casinos, bars, and even gyms for its 555 passengers.

Around the World in 39 Days

Mohammed Salahuddin Choudhury and his wife Neena of Calcutta, India, circumnavigated the Earth by car in just 39 days. They completed their record-breaking journey in Delhi in 1991.

Close Encounters

In 1996, Nevada State Route 375 was officially named the "Extraterrestrial Highway" by the Nevada Governor, Bob Miller. The highway is, apparently, one of the most "visited" in the country.

Monster Mash

"Bigfoot" is the biggest monster truck in the world: it is 15 ft 5 in (4.7 m) tall, weighs 38,000 lb (17,000 kg) and has 10-ft (3-m) high tires. It was made by Bob Chandler of St. Louis, Missouri.

A Real Hummer-dinger
It's 39 ft (12 m) long, 8.5 ft (2.5 m) wide, and it costs £1,000 ($1,900) a night to hire—it's Britain's longest stretch limousine, a Hummer, owned by Scott Demaret of Bristol.

Arriving in Style
Inside, chilled drinks on tap, luxurious leather seating, and air-conditioning make bumpy rides a thing of the past.

My Hands Are Tied

In 2004, Italian Alberto Cristini swam the 2 mi (3 km) from the island of Alcatraz to San Francisco in 1 hour, 50 minutes—with his hands and feet tied together! Fighting strong currents, Alberto, who lives near Venice, made it through the freezing cold stretch of water. The race was pioneered in 1955 by fitness guru Jack La Lanne, who did it while wearing handcuffs.

Plane Stupid

Louis Kadlecek had never flown a plane, but stole a two-seater Cessna from an airport in Houston, Texas, and flew for about a mile before crashing into electricity lines. Mr. Kadlecek was unhurt and walked home after the accident, before being arrested by police.

Just Deserts

The Baja 1,000 Desert Race takes place every November. It's a famous test of endurance, during which car drivers have been known to cover the very bumpy 1,000-mi (1,500-km) course with broken bones. Ivan "Ironman" Stewart completed the course in just 20 hours in 1998.

The Flip Side

At the Gravity Games in Rhode Island, in 2002, Carey Hart performed a back flip on a motorbike, traveling 20 ft (6 m) before landing. It was the first recorded back flip on a full-size bike.

Judge Dread

Officials in Mount Holly, New Jersey, decided to introduce humorous road signs because the conventional kind were not proving to be effective enough. The colorful signs bear messages such as "Meet Our Judge—Exceed 25 mph (40 km/h)" and "Free Speeding Tickets Ahead."

Chuting Star

In his lifetime, Henry ("Cloudbuster Hen") Langer ascended in an aircraft 479 times but never once landed in a plane—instead, he parachuted back to Earth every time.

U.S.A.
New York

Citizens may not greet each other by "putting one's thumb to the nose and wiggling the fingers."

Motor Boat
In 1999, a rather unusual vehicle was licensed to travel on the roads. Englishman John Brown customized his Robin Reliant car and a Mombar speedboat. Now the road-legal watercraft doesn't have to stop at Land's End!

Oar-inspiring
Measuring 140 ft (42 m) and weighing 2,200 lb (1,000 kg), the world's longest rowing boat requires 24 rowers.

Jam Session
In 1864, in order to get to work in Peublo, Colorado, school teacher Clara Weston waded across the Arkansas river twice a day for four months.

Putting a Spoke in her Wheels
In 2004, police who were raiding the home of a woman in Berlin, Germany, found no fewer than 78 stolen bicycles stacked in high piles.

The Good Ship Lollipop
In 2003, Robert McDonald from Emmeloord, Holland, stayed afloat for 19 minutes on a boat made out of 370,000 lollipop sticks. The experience has inspired him to plan the construction of a 50-ft (15-m) replica Viking longship made from 15 million lollipop sticks, in which he one day hopes to sail across the Atlantic.

Ups and Downs

WHEN RICHARD RODRIQUEZ began his attempt to break the world record for riding on a roller coaster, he had no idea he would take 2,000 rides during the year 2000!

In his latest attempt to break a record, Richard Rodriguez has so far spent a quarter of a year on a roller coaster!

Bumpy Ride
Al McKee covered 45,000 mi (67,500 km) during 60,000 trips on one roller coaster—he was the driver of the scenic railway ride at New Jersey's Palisades Amusement Park.

The university lecturer from Chicago, Illinois, performed all 2,000 rides on the same Big Dipper in Blackpool, England, and timed each ride to see how fast he could go. When asked what he did to pass the time while on the Big Dipper, he said he sent text messages and read books and newspapers.

Cheap Thrills

John Ivers of Bruceville, Indiana, likes roller coasters so much that he has built one in his backyard. Blue Flash, the 180-ft (55-m) long, 20-ft (6-m) high ride, wraps round his barn and a tree. It cost just $1,500 (£775) and has a top speed of 25 mph (40 km/h).

Golden Wedding

When the Sultan of Brunei's son got married in September 2004, the wedding car was a $20 million (£10 million), gold-encrusted stretch Rolls-Royce. The luxury car was open-topped to accommodate a double throne for Crown Prince Al-Muhtadee Billah Bolkiah and his bride Sarah Salleh. Since even money couldn't buy perfect weather, a golden umbrella was fitted to the car to protect the couple from the rain.

U.S.A. New York

While riding in an elevator, it is illegal for one to talk to another, or to fold one's hands while looking toward the door.

Race Relations

The island of Tobago hosts annual goat and crab races. Goat jockeys run around the race track alongside the goats, while the crabs are harnessed with string and encouraged along their course by prods from their jockeys.

Pajama Party

Every January, American bed-racing enthusiasts flock to Arizona for the annual Oatman Bed Race. Following a nightwear parade, the teams push their beds down the main street, make their beds, and then race back to the finish line... all to the sweet sounds of the Chamber Pot Band. Even burly bikers have been known to swap their leathers for fluffy pajamas.

Elementary, My Dear Watson

Lloyd Scott, a former British soccer player, used a big-wheeled penny farthing bicycle to cross the continent of Australia in the fall 2004. Scott's 2,700-mi (4,500-km) ride from Perth to Sydney—dressed as Sherlock Holmes—was estimated to have raised almost $2.7 million (£1.4 million) for charity.

He Swims Like a Fish

Brazilian Jose Martins Ribeiro Nunes, who is also known as "Ze Peixe" or "the fish," is 74 years old and leads an exceptionally active life—he guides ships in and out of Brazil's port by swimming along in front of them. He often swims about 8 mi (12 km), in extremely choppy waters, to guide the vessels safely into and out of the harbor! Jose's lifestyle has made him famous on land and at sea, all over the world.

On Home Ground

A river steamer that ran aground off Sauries Island, near Portland, Oregon, was turned into a houseboat.

Tanks a Million

On his 265-acre (107-ha) estate, Texas millionaire David Estes uses 25 military tanks to teach corporate employees leadership through his company, Tactical Tanks. One important lesson participants learn is about communication, because Estes intentionally creates chaos, disinformation, and ambiguity in the activities to test them.

Pay Day

It took decades, but an Arizona man has finally paid a $1 (50p) parking ticket 38 years after he received it. He found the ticket in an old box that he'd carted around through moves in more than six states and decided it was high time to pay up.

All the Fun of the Fair

Max Tate of Newcastle, England, has converted a fairground bumper car into a street-legal vehicle capable of speeds of 90 mph (145 km/h).

Shoe Tree

On Highway 50 near Middle Gate, Nevada, a lone cottonwood tree is draped with hundreds of pairs of shoes thrown over the branches by passers-by. The first pair are said to have been tossed there during a wedding-night row between young newlyweds.

Slow Coaches

A group of Indiana high school seniors drove so slowly in traffic—at approximately 15 mph (25 km/h)—as a prank, that police cited them for reckless driving. The officers were miffed because the students' low speeds caused a 60-car back-up on an Indiana freeway that took the officers 20 minutes to clear up.

Going Like a Rocket

Billy Copeland rode his rocket-powered skateboard at 70 mph (113 km/h) in 1998, setting a world record.

**U.S.A.
North Dakota**

In Fargo, one may be jailed for wearing a hat while dancing, or even for wearing a hat to a function where dancing is taking place.

Carted Around

Andy Tyler of Suffolk, England, has created the world's fastest shopping cart—by fitting it with a jet engine! Powered by gas and liquid fuel, it can reach speeds of over 50 mph (80 km/h). There are drawbacks. In order to propel the cart, the engine explodes 40 times a second and is so noisy that it hurts Andy's ears—and he's unlikely ever to be allowed to take it round his local supermarket!

Moving Home
This brick house in Palm Beach, Florida, was donated to a children's charity and moved in one piece to its new location by truck and by barge.

Hair-raising
Entrepreneur Pat Nevin has just the thing for kids to give their parents a shock—his "Hairy Helmets" are colored mohawks that he velcros on to bicycle helmets. He hopes Harley riders might like to try his styles too.

Baby You Can Drive My Car
According to a car survey by Yahoo!Autos, U.S. freeways may be a better place to meet people than weddings or bars, as 62 percent admitted that they love to flirt behind the wheel—and that they are more attracted to those who drive nicer cars.

Holy Roller
In the 1970s, it was not unusual to see this mobile church on Britain's roads. The brainchild of one Reverend Dunlop, it was an ordinary bus that was painted to look like a church, complete with a spire sticking out of the roof.

Disco to Go

Anyone hailing a taxi in Aspen, Colorado, could be in for an unusual journey. For Jon Barnes' Ultimate Taxi offers a ride complete with disco ball, smoke machine, strobe lights, lasers, and a dry-ice machine. As if that wasn't enough, there's even a drum kit, keyboard, digital camera, and a gift shop in the trunk.

We Have Lift Off!

ON OCTOBER 4, 2004, SpaceShipOne rocketed into history, becoming the first private, manned spacecraft to exceed an altitude of 328,000 ft (100,000 m)!

In doing so—twice within a two-week period—team members claimed the $10 million (£5 million) Ansari X Prize in an international competition designed to spur civilian spaceflight. The competition included seven teams from the U.S.A., as well as groups from Argentina, Canada, Romania, the U.K., and Russia.

The SpaceShipOne team members launched themselves into the record books with their successful private space flight.

Seeing Stars

The fastest-ever spacecraft were two German probes. They were launched from Cape Canaveral, in Florida, and reached 158,000 mph (254,280 km/h) during their orbit of the Sun.

215

Couch Potatoes

It may look like any old sofa, but this one can reach speeds of up to 87 mph (140 km/h)! Licensed for use on U.K. roads, it was created by inventors Edd China and David Davenport, and is powered by a 1300cc engine. The steering-wheel is made out of a medium-sized pizza pan and the brake pedal is a cola can.

Put Your Foot in It

A veteran skydiver got his foot caught outside an airplane door and it dangled there in the Pittsburgh skies for 30 minutes. He was still hanging upon landing, but wasn't hurt.

In the Pink

Janette Hanson of Macclesfield, England, paid £10,000 ($20,000) to have her Mini Cooper customized—just so that it matched her £20 ($40) handbag! She wanted the new car to be an exact match for her pink bag and splashed out the extra cash for the pink finish and trim.

Bubble, Bubble...

Heavy rains in August 2004 created a bubblefest in Dunn, North Carolina, thanks to soap-based run-off from a factory. A 20-ft (6-m) tall wall of white bubbles obscured the road, but some drivers tried to navigate the mess. Smart ones waited until local firefighters tamed the foam with their hoses.

Chainsaws Massacred

This unusual stretch motorbike is powered by 24 chainsaws.

Power Napping

Englishman Edd China specializes in weird vehicles. For £100 ($195), he takes tourists around London on a motorized four-poster bed. The bed, welded to a 1,600cc Volkswagen engine, has insurance, and all legal road-testing, and was inspired by the 1960s TV series *The Monkees*. "It cost £5,000 ($9,700) and took two months to build," says Ed, "but it impresses the women!" He also drives a bath and a motorized sofa.

Tough Luck

A 17-year-old teenager from Washington survived a car crash that left her trapped down a ravine in her car for eight days. Doctors think that dehydration may have saved her life, as it stopped a blood clot in her brain from expanding. When she was found by an acquaintance, she said she felt led to the site by a dream.

Going Solo

The world's smallest street-legal car was produced on Britain's Isle of Man in the 1960s. The Peel P50 was 53 in (135 cm) high, 53 in (135 cm) long, and 39 in (100 cm) wide. It carried one adult and could reach a top speed of 40 mph (65 km/h).

Home from Home

Charles Miller of Portland, Oregon, created domestic bliss in the back of his truck. The vehicle he made home was 3 ft 9 in (1 m) wide and 6 ft (1.8 m) long, and he toured the country clocking up more than 200,000 mi (300,000 km) on the way.

High Jinx

Certain street signs in Eugene, Oregon, routinely get stolen by students attending the University of Oregon as decoration for their rooms. The sign for High Street has been replaced nearly 350 times in the last decade, and the city has spent at least $50,000 (£26,000) on new signs in the last year alone.

Learner Driver

An 11-year-old Kansas City boy, who had previously driven only a tractor, took off on a 200-mi (300-km) trip in the family car after being involved in an argument at his school. At one point he ran out of gas, but some construction workers helped him to refuel. However, his big adventure finally stalled when he locked himself out of the car after taking a break. His parents sent him straight back to school the very next day.

In Distress

After an Oregon man's television began emitting the international distress signal (the 121.5 megahertz beep emitted by crashed airplanes and sinking boats), the Air Force, a county search-and-rescue deputy, and the police arrived at his door. The distress signal had been picked up by a satellite, relayed to an Air Force base in Virginia, on to the Civil Air Patrol, and finally to officials in Oregon. The man hurried to replace his TV as he didn't want to pay a $10,000 (£5,000) daily fine should his old set pipe up again.

Drinking and Driving

In 2003, Tony Anchors, from Didcot, England, wanted to do something completely different with his Mini—so he converted it into a mobile bar!

Was That A Good Idea?

Inflated Innovation!

NOW HERE'S AN invention you can drink to—the first inflatable pub!

The traveling tavern can hold up to 30 visitors at a time. English designer Andi Francis worked on the idea for nine months after deciding to create a drinks marquee with a bit more flare than a beer tent.

The interior of the blow-up bar has everything you might expect in the real thing. It comes complete with fireplace (which is, of course, purely decorative), a stuffed fish mounted on one wall, mock Tudor beams, and lattice windows.

The Pub

Hot-desking
OIAB (Office in a Bucket) is the ideal solution for any company boss wanting to give his staff a change of scenery. Simply pick your spot—maybe the park or even the beach—and the office can be inflated in just eight minutes.

Blue Sky Thinking
The inflatable office can be inflated wherever you like—in parks, gardens, or even on a rooftop—to provide workers with a change of scenery and fresh inspiration every day.

Out of Sight
Henry Bayerl of Portsmouth, Ohio, managed to completely overhaul a car while wearing a blindfold.

Breach of the Peace
A concert composed by Luciano Berio was once held to promote world peace. Halfway through the concert, a cannon was fired that injured several people in the audience and then caused a riot to break out.

Big Shot
One time when General George Custer was hunting buffalo, he accidentally shot his own horse!

Cutting Corners
Sami Sure, a construction worker in Beirut, Lebanon, couldn't afford to pay his barber 65 cents (35 pence) for a shave, so he gave him half of his lottery ticket instead. The ticket won and the barber scooped $133,000 (£70,500).

From a Scream to a Whisper
Ever wanted to scream out loud during a stressful situation? Well now you can with an invention that allows the "stressee" to shout into a small ball that is filled with special foam that muffles the noise, making it seem like a whisper.

Bullet-proof Pizza
When Cole Woolner of Michigan was delivering two deep-dish pizzas, his life was saved—by the pizzas! A bullet hit the pies and missed him.

Pup, Pup, and Away
Buddy the Labrador and his owner, Bill Kimball of San Diego, California, have been hang-gliding together for more than eight years. Buddy's first flight took place when he was a six-month-old pup. Since then, he has joined Bill on more than 75 flights.

Give and Take

In 1795, Boston millionaire James Swan paid off the American national debt to France, a total of $2,024,900 (£1,072,700), from his own pocket! However, he spent the last 22 years of his life in jail, as the French government sent him to Saint Pelagie Prison for debtors.

Mississippi Blues

Instead of taking his vehicle to a proper car wash, a man from Hannibal, Missouri, decided to save money by cleaning it in the nearby Mississippi River. He carefully backed it into a foot of water, but when he got out to start washing it, the car floated away. The police later recovered it some way downstream.

Blowing Hot and Cold

A British man got more than he bargained for when his lips became stuck to the lock on his car door while he was blowing on it in order to defrost it!

Gone Fishing

The "Aquariass," which attaches to a working toilet, is a quirky cistern fitted with a real aquarium. But don't worry, the fish aren't actually flushed away!

Name Dropping

Cleston Jenkins of Kentucky had the first names of each of his seven ex-wives tattooed on his arm.

Money Matters

In April 2000, the Brazilian government issued bank-notes made of plastic!

Eyes Like a Hawk

An excited birdwatcher used CB radio to bring twitchers flocking to a field on the Isles of Scilly, off the southwest of England, to see a nighthawk, a rare visitor from America. Only when telescopes and binoculars were trained on it did it become apparent that the "rare bird" was in fact a cowpat!

Musical Chairs

Some people sing in the shower, some even sing on the toilet, but fancy having a toilet sing to you! This singing loo, by Swiss inventors Reto Marogg and Roger Weisskopf, was presented at the annual exhibition of inventions in Geneva.

Talk is Cheap

Unable to find a summer job, teenager Trevor Dame tried to earn money by giving out advice on a street corner in his hometown of Kelowna, British Columbia. Aware that his advice might not be of the highest quality, he wore a sign around his neck saying, "Mediocre advice—25 cents."

Wake-up Call

In 1907, a patent was filed for an alarm clock that sprays water on the face of a sleeping person.

Get Back to Your Roots

Scientists developed these multi-colored carrots to encourage more people to eat their vegetables. Not only that, but the modified carrots are actually better for you, due to the healthy pigments used to change their color.

Clean and Sober

After stealing cash from a Colorado Springs corner store, an armed robber demanded a bottle of whiskey from the shelf. The clerk refused to serve him because he didn't believe he was 21. To prove he was, the robber obligingly showed the clerk his driver's licence—bearing his full name and address.

U.S.A.
Oklahoma

It is illegal for women to do their own hair without being licensed by the state.

Snake Bite
Jack Bibby actually put live rattlesnakes in his mouth.

Cuddling Up

IF YOU'RE USED to a cuddle at bedtime, these pillows might help for nights when you're alone.

Made in Japan, the Lap Pillow and My Boyfriend's Arm Pillow are designed for those who are most comfortable sleeping next to someone else. They help you to sleep by simulating the shape of an absent loved-one.

The Lap Pillow is shaped like a kneeling woman and comes with either a red or black skirt.

Playing with Fire

Bestselling children's novelist, G.P. Taylor accidentally burned three of his manuscripts. While clearing out his house in preparation for moving, Taylor mistook the original manuscripts for old paperwork and burned them to cinders. One of them, which had gone on to sell in excess of 250,000 copies, was given a £100,000 ($190,000) value by a collector prior to the incident.

The manuscripts Taylor accidentally burned were for three of his bestselling novels: Shadowmancer, Wormwood, *and* Tersias.

The Finger of Suspicion

When arrested in 2003, a Nigerian man chewed off his own fingertips so his prints couldn't be taken. He soaked his fingers in the jail toilet, then chewed away the softened skin.

Early Warning System

A man went into a McDonald's in Sydney, Australia, at 8.50 a.m. one day in 2000, produced a gun and demanded cash. The girl serving said she couldn't open the till without a food order. So the robber ordered a Big Mac, but was told that they weren't available until 10.30 because only the breakfast menu was being offered at that time. Frustrated, the gunman gave up and walked out.

An Unscheduled Flight

An airport baggage-handler made an unscheduled flight from Dallas to Mexico in 2001 after accidentally locking himself in the plane's cargo hold. Crew members reported hearing a knocking sound at Dallas, but weren't able to trace it.

Pulling a Fast One

A 41-year-old man from Barrie, Canada, who pretended to be a traffic policeman was sentenced to six months in jail after pulling over a real detective for speeding.

Pot Shot

J.G. Levack, an exhibition shooter from Connecticut, tossed a golf ball in the air and hit it with a rifle bullet. He did this with such accuracy that it landed on a green with 150 yd (137 m) distance.

Finger Stuck

An Illinois man who got his finger stuck in a payphone for three hours was taken to the hospital with the phone still attached to his hand. Passers-by, fire crews, and a workman from the phone company all failed to free him, until, eventually, paramedics cut the phone from its base and took the man—and the phone—to the hospital.

Natural Wastage

Government officials in Sydney, Nova Scotia, spent $410,000 (£215,000) erecting a fence topped with barbed-wire around a toxic-waste site in 2001. Since they fixed it so that the barbed-wire faced inward, the fence allowed easy access to the hazardous site but then trapped trespassers inside!

By Hook or by Crook

A 36-year-old man who robbed an Ontario discount store was quickly arrested, mainly because he made no attempt to disguise the metal hook that he used in place of a hand.

A Lingering Kiss

A pair of teenagers kissing in their car at traffic lights in Rio de Janeiro held up traffic for two-and-a-half hours when their dental braces became entwined.

By the Skin of his Teeth
Sri Lankan farmer Gamini Wasantha Kumara displays extraordinary pulling power. Gamini is seen here biting down on a harness in preparation for his train-pulling challenge at Colombo's main railway station in 2001.

In Training

Gamini Wasantha Kumara pulled the 40-ton railway carriage a total of more than 80 ft (25 m) in Colombo, Sri Lanka, using only the harness gripped between his teeth!

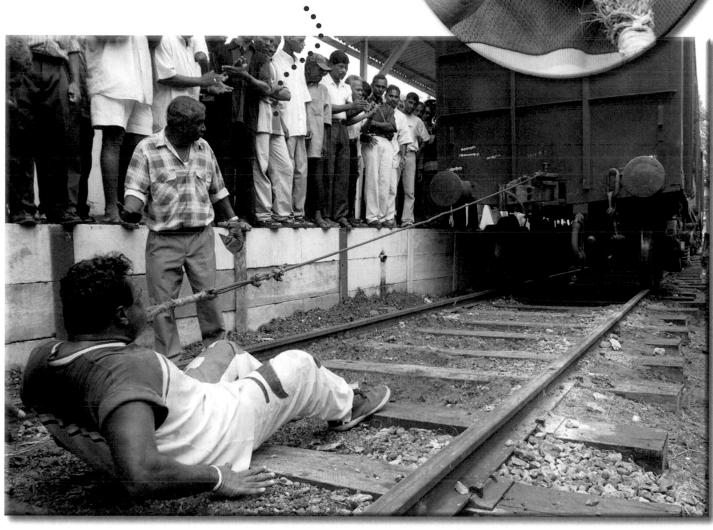

Duty Calls

Passengers on a flight from Zurich, Switzerland, to London panicked when it was announced that the plane was about to crash in the ocean. Then the captain explained that they had played the wrong tape: "We meant to tell you we were about to serve the duty-free products," he said.

Sleeping Partner

In 2002, a Romanian pensioner ran up a bill of £950 ($1,800)—the equivalent of the average annual salary in Romania—after falling asleep while on a phone chat line.

Log Jam

Kenneth Lambert of New Hampshire crossed the log-jammed Androscoggin River on snow skis.

Opening Shelved

In Gloucestershire, England, a council had to inform residents that a new £2 million ($3.7 million) library would not be opening on schedule in 2003 because the council had forgotten to order any books or shelves!

Under the Knife

A man from Chino Valley, Arizona, who had been playing with a knife by tossing it into the air, was taken to hospital with a 12-in (30-cm) steak knife firmly embedded in the back of his head.

The Milk of Human Kindness

A woman in Nanjin, China, ordered 3,000 barrels of milk over a three-month period in the name of a local university as she feared that her boyfriend, a dairy company sales manager, would be recalled to their head office due to poor milk sales.

Balancing Act
A.C. Johnson of Kansas balanced an egg on a piece of chicken wire.

Taking the Plunge

DIVING 29 FT (9 m) into water may not sound too challenging, but it certainly is when the water is only 12 in (30 cm) deep!

Louisiana-born diver Danny Higginbottom took the plunge in front of spectators in London, England, and earned himself a place in the record books for his splashing feat!

Injury Time

There were so many injuries during 2004's Women's National Festival of Rugby in Staffordshire, England, that emergency services termed it "a major incident." Ten ambulances and a helicopter dealt with ruptured muscles, broken bones, and even a dislocated hip.

Double Bass
Arthur K. Ferris of Ironia, New Jersey, built a 14-ft (4.25-m) high bass fiddle.

Hide and Seek

A British woman sparked a full-scale police search, complete with helicopter, for her three-year-old daughter in 2004... when the child was behind a couch the whole time. It was estimated that the search cost £30,000 ($57,000).

Blast Off

Wanting a gas stove for her apartment, a San Francisco woman stole one from a neighboring building... without first turning off the gas. She caused a $200,000 (£105,000) explosion.

Break a Leg

Charles Grubbs and Melody Wyman had set their hearts on being married at the top of Mount Rainier, Washington State, but on their way up the mountain for the 2002 ceremony, high winds blew them and their minister into a crevasse. After a visit to hospital, the wedding went ahead as planned... except that the bride had a plaster cast on her leg and needed the aid of a crutch.

Blank Looks

A counterfeiter in Paramount, California, did a sterling job preparing fake notes that he tried to pass on to a store owner. There was just one giveaway: the back of the bills was completely blank.

What a Giveaway

Los Angeles police got lucky with a robbery suspect who just couldn't keep his mouth shut. When detectives asked each man in the line-up to repeat the words, "Give me all your money or I'll shoot," the guilty man shouted: "That's not what I said!"

U.S.A.
Ohio

Any map that does not have Lima clearly stated on it cannot be sold.

Breaking the Ice

Sri Lankan farmer Gamini Wasantha Kumara endured having no fewer than 50 blocks of ice dropped on him from a height of 17 ft (5 m). Gamini laid with a block of granite weighing 440 lb (200 kg) on his chest, while the blocks of ice, each weighing a further 110 lb (50 kg), were dropped on top of him, one at a time.

Gamini Wasantha Kumara has made several attempts to get into Ripley's record books with his various feats.

Between a Rock and a Hard Place
No stranger to heights or handstands, Eskil Ronningsbakken balances on four stacked chairs at more than 3,000 ft (1,000 m) above sea level in Norway.

Hit the Roof
Extreme artist Eskil Ronningsbakken does a handstand on top of the 280-ft (86-m) high Radisson S.A.S. Scandinavia Building in Copenhagen, Denmark.

Real Cliffhanger
Eskil Ronningsbakken performing his trademark handstand without a safety net 2,000 ft (600 m) above sea level at Pulpit Cliff, Norway.

It's in the Bag

Hoping to look inconspicuous, a bank robber in Portland, Oregon, handed the teller a note ordering her to put all the money in a paper bag. She read the note, wrote on the bottom, "I don't have a paper bag," and handed it back to the raider. His plan foiled, he fled empty-handed.

Topple That!
Captain W. E. Wyatt from Fort Worth, Texas, used 84 dominoes for this feat in 1931. The steady-handed police officer managed to stack 83 dominoes on top of the single vertical one!

When You're in a Hole...

After six months of digging a secret tunnel from Saltillo Prison, Mexico, 75 convicts made their daring bid for freedom, only to find that their tunnel emerged in the nearby courtroom where many of them had been sentenced. The surprised judges quickly sent them back to jail.

Mummy's Boy

A 22-year-old Los Angeles man advertised in a magazine as a lonely Romeo looking for a girl to accompany him on vacation to South America. Alas, the first reply he received turned out to be from his widowed mother!

Badge of Dishonor

A would-be robber of a Texas grocery store disguised his face with a balaclava, but forgot to remove from his breast pocket a laminated badge that bore his name, place of employment, and position within the company—an oversight spotted by witnesses.

Lost in Translation

An elderly American tourist had to be rescued from woodland in Bavaria, Germany, in 2004 after he got lost while using a 90-year-old guidebook.

Get your Facts Straight

A woman from Connecticut was identified in 2003 as the person who had robbed six banks only after she called her local newspaper to complain about inaccuracies in their reports of her robberies.

What's the Hold-up?

A man robbed a bank in Briarwood, West Virginia, in 2004 by taping a "stick-up" note to the teller's window. He was arrested when he later returned to the same window because he had forgotten to pick up the note!

Seed Drill

Taiwanese artist Chen Frong-Shean wrote this 28-character poem by ancient Chinese poet Su Tung-po on a sesame seed! When the seed is placed on the face of George Washington on a $1 note, the scale of the writing can be fully appreciated.

No Strings Attached
Contortionist Captain Frodo, a member of the Circus Oz, dislocates certain bones in his body to enable him to pass his body through a tennis racket as part of his performance!

Turn Yourself In

After robbing an Ohio convenience store in 2004, a man hijacked a car and led police on a high-speed chase before taking a wrong turn and driving into a police station parking lot.

A Sight to Remember

Residents of the Romanian village of Cristinesti fled their homes in panic in 2004 after mistaking disco lights in a nearby town for an alien invasion!

Finger of Fate

A man in Modesto, California, was arrested for trying to hold up a Bank of America branch without a weapon. He used a thumb and finger to simulate a gun, but forgot to keep his hand in his pocket.

Airline Food

A group of vintage aviation enthusiasts left their plane in a field near Hereford, England, while they went to lunch in a nearby pub. When they returned, they found the 1948 Auster airplane being eaten by cows! The animals caused thousands of pounds of damage by chewing a large hole in the fuselage.

Bent Out of Shape

DONALD HAMBLY can bend iron bars using only his neck!

Putting great faith in the Shaolin monk meditation he practices, Donald positions the bars against his throat and gradually moves forward, bending them as he goes.

The steel rods could puncture Donald's throat at any time during the act, but his skill and concentration ensure his safety.

To begin with, the bars are moved into place and Donald starts to push!

He stays tense and alert as the bars gradually bend in the middle.

It starts to give as he applies pressure against the bars.

One final push toward the end, and he's almost there!

235

Stone the Crows!

Mistaking it for a Viking settlement, archeologists excavated an ordinary 1940s patio in a back garden in Fife, Scotland.

Other Fish to Fry

Firefighters in Baton Rouge, Louisiana, burned down their own fire station after leaving fish frying on a stove when they were called out to attend a blaze.

A Hiding to Nothing

A Romanian man sentenced for fraud in 1994 hid in his parents' basement for eight years—to avoid a three-and-a-half-year jail sentence.

Unlucky Number

Sentenced to seven years in jail, a man from San Antonio, Texas, begged the judge not to give him seven years because seven was his unlucky number. So the judge gave him eight years.

Caught Out

Two burglars fled from a building in Florida in 2003 and jumped into what they thought was their getaway car, only to find that it was an unmarked police car!

Barbie World

As part of a promotion for Barbie, all the houses in this street in Manchester, England, were temporarily painted bright pink!

A Nasty Shock

A man in Kitwe, Zambia, was electrocuted in 2000 when, having run out of space on his clothes line, he unwisely decided to hang the remainder of his wet washing on a live power line that passed his house.

Double Trouble

A year after crashing into Jim Hughes' yacht near Portsmouth, England, and causing £20,000 ($40,000) damage, Icelandic sailor Eriker Olafsson still felt guilty. So he decided to return to the harbor and make a full apology, only to hit Mr Hughes' yacht again and postpone his plans for a round-the-world voyage for a second time!

A Cut Above
Joe Horowitz from Los Angeles was able to balance an 18-lb (8-kg) saber on the end of his nose!

Courtroom Drama

A computer error resulted in an eight-year-old boy from New Jersey being summoned for jury service in 2001. It was the second time Kyle Connor had been called up to serve on a jury, the first being when he was five. Kyle said he was perfectly happy to try it, so long as the judge didn't mind!

Tooth and Nail

A dentist soon got to the root of Patrick Lawler's toothache—a 4-in (10-cm) nail that the construction worker had embedded in his skull six days earlier! A nail gun had backfired while he was working at a Colorado ski resort, sending one nail into a piece of wood, and another through his mouth and 1.5 in (4 cm) into his brain.

Triumphant Stag

An American poacher who shot a stag standing above him on an overhanging rock was killed instantly when the dead animal fell on him.

Wind Break

Frank Morosky of Cedar Rapids, Iowa, has made charcoal-lined diapers costing between $20 (£10) and $50 (£25), to reduce the odor of dogs' flatulence.

Puss in... Slippers

Japanese inventor Kenji Kawakami has conceived a pair of duster slippers to be worn by a cat, so that the animal can polish the floor while it walks!

On the Record

A pair of agitated robbers burst into a record store in Michigan, nervously waving guns. One shouted: "Nobody move!" When his accomplice moved, the first bandit shot him.

Denmark
Attempting to escape from prison is not actually illegal, although if recaptured, one is required to serve out the remainder of one's term.

Bare-faced Cheek

A Canadian man who was refused a ticket from Los Angeles to Australia in 2004, took off all his clothes, ran naked across the runway, and climbed into a plane's wheel well. Firefighters finally talked him out.

The Party's Over

After a party in 2001, a woman fell asleep on a mattress in an Alabama garbage bin... and woke hours later in a Georgia landfill 20 mi (30 km) away. She narrowly escaped being crushed by a garbage compactor.

Heavy Duty
Weighing 147 lb (67 kg), Stephen Stoyan made two successive push-ups with 285 lb (129 kg) on his back.

237

Pressing the Limits

REV. JON BRUNEY from Fremont, Indiana, performs radical exhibitions of strength as part of his "Pressing the Limits" event.

His strongman activities include breaking flaming bricks, crushing a full can of soda, and inflating a hot-water bottle until it explodes. In July 2004, Jon was one of three strongmen to pull a 15-ton semi-tractor trailer for a distance of 1 mi (1.5 km)! The trailer was loaded with the band, Bledsoe, who performed on the flatbed of the truck.

Jon lays under a bed of 3,000 nails, as a woman jumps rope on top of the wooden board. Afterward, the audience could see nail indentations in Jon's skin, but no sign of more serious physical injury.

Jon Bruney bends a steel bar against the top of his head, during one of his motivational performances.

To illustrate his sheer strength, Jon is able to tear entire phone books in half!

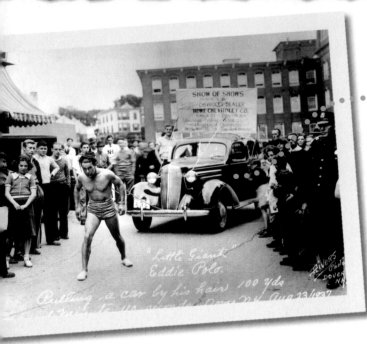

Tearing his Hair Out

"Little Giant" Eddie Polo pulls a car 100 yd (90 m) in 1 minute 40 seconds in Dover, New Hampshire, in August 1931—using only the strength of his hair.

Economy Drive

Resenting the prospect of paying a $55 (£30) delivery fee on his new lawnmower, a man from Plainville, Connecticut, decided instead to drive it home along the road at a top speed of 12 mph (20 km/h). Far from saving money, he was fined $78 (£40) for driving an unregistered vehicle!

A Lost Cause

A tourist from Toledo, Washington, on holiday in Germany in 2003, relied solely on his car's automatic navigation system to steer him around the unfamiliar roads of Bavaria... until it led him straight through the doors of a supermarket. The tourist, who said he didn't even see the supermarket doors, came to a halt when he crashed into shelves.

Life's a Beach

One bank of the River Seine is turned into a beach each summer so that Parisians can enjoy the sunshine without having to trek to the coast. The mayor had the "Paris Plage" developed to include palm trees, sand, and a swimming pool.

Growing Room

A German firm has developed a shoe that grows to keep pace with children's feet. At the press of a button, the shoe increases by one size by expanding like an accordion.

On the Fiddle

Ontario police charged a motorist with careless driving after catching him playing the violin while driving. The 54-year-old man said he was warming up for a concert.

Having a Ball

The Stade de France stadium in Paris was transformed into a beach in July 2002 with 100,000 sq ft (9,000 sq m) of sand. Visitors could play ball games or simply relax in deckchairs.

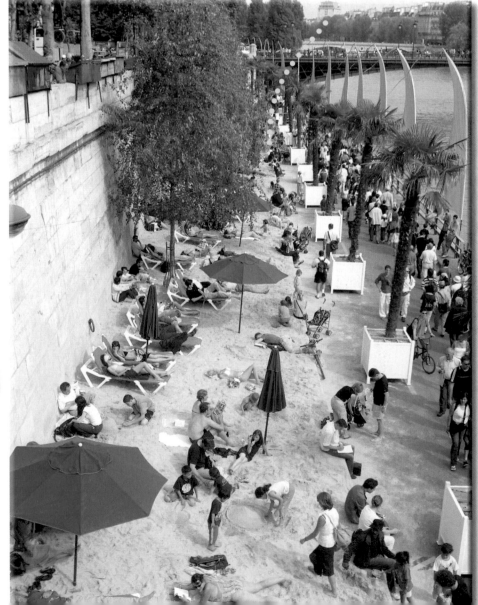

Bear the BLow

IF BASEBALL BATS and cars are no match for this super suit, then a grizzly bear doesn't stand much chance of getting through either!

Troy Hurtibuse of North Bay, Canada, tested the strength of his specially made protective suit at the Ripley's museum in St. Augustine, Florida.

The suit is designed to help nature photographers get closer than ever before to bears in the wild, without the fear of being mauled by them.

The tests Troy's suit endured included being hit repeatedly with steel baseball bats by members of the audience, and even being hit by a swinging car! Troy is seen here sitting among a pile of bricks that were previously a wall. The car was swung at him and hit him in the chest. He was knocked down but otherwise unhurt, while the wall was smashed.

Coffee Break

Civet coffee was developed as a luxurious option for the adventurous. The coffee is processed in the digestive tract from the civet cat of Sumatra. The cat eats the coffee beans, which are then hand-picked from its droppings. The coffee costs the princely sum of £14 ($26) for an ounce because only 1,100 lb (500 kg) of it are made every year. However, experts genuinely enjoy the taste. One Dutch connoisseur described it as having a fine chocolate aroma that gives a delicious taste at the back of the throat.

Even if you're a coffee-lover, you might have the same reaction as this when you discover how civet coffee is made!

The Name of the Game

When Californian artist Maria Alquilar painted a $40,000 (£21,000) mural outside a public library, little did she realize that it contained 11 misspelled names of historical giants including Einstein, Shakespeare, Van Gogh, and Michelangelo. It is thought to have cost around $6,000 (£3,000) to correct the mistakes.

O Brother!

Acting as his own lawyer in a Texas federal court, Adam Martin called his brother to the witness stand to testify to his good character. When Adam asked his brother if he had ever committed any crimes, his brother responded without hesitation: "Yeah. You were with me on four different bank robberies, Adam. You know that."

Heaven Scent

These rose-scented stamps were used on letters in Thailand in 2002. Printed in England, they were released in Bangkok in February to commemorate St. Valentine's Day.

A Change of Key

Frankie Masters had a 12-stong band, with a difference—each member played music on a manual typewriter. The overall effect sounded like a xylophone.

Banana Split

A Cincinnati-based firm is planning to market strawberry-flavored bananas! Chiquita International claims bananas taste boring.

Dozy Burglar

It was bad enough that a burglar chose to break into the offices of the police department in Oxnard, California, but to make matters worse, he then fell asleep! Bemused police discovered him when they arrived for work in the morning, and promptly made him the first arrest of the day.

I Want to Ride My Tricycle

Bobby Jordan and six of his friends, who call themselves the "Descanso Big Wheel Boys," consider themselves Big Wheel daredevils—despite being adults. For the last year, the full-grown men have been getting their thrills by racing their toy tricycles down steep California mountainsides. They typically reach 35 mph (55 km/h), which causes the plastic wheels to disintegrate long before they reach the bottom.

Going to the Dogs

Tina and Kate, two dogs living in Somerset, England, inherited £450,000 ($850,000) when their owner passed away. The inheritance was enough for them to be able to enjoy a home and 4 acre (1.6 ha) of land in the village of Peasedown St. John.

Brace Yourself

Truck driver Herbert Scott from Burnley, England, in 1986 sought medical attention following a fall at work. As a result of a misunderstanding, he kept a neck brace on for the next 14 years instead of the four weeks that the doctors had advised.

Bird Brained

Thieves who stole 15 homing pigeons from bird-fancier Peter Ball of Berkshire, England, tried them out... and watched in despair as they flew straight back to Ball's loft!

The Color of Money

An unemployed American printer who turned to counterfeiting was caught because he used black ink instead of bright green on his phoney bills. It turned out that he was color-blind.

Fire Drill

When fire broke out at a restaurant in the Austrian city of Vienna in November 2003, the owner and staff quickly fled the building. In their haste, they forgot to evacuate the guests. Even though the dining-room had filled with smoke, 20 people were still sitting at their tables when fire crews arrived.

It's a Dog's Life

These lucky pups are now looked after by gardener Henry Escott, who ensures that they have everything they need.

Giving Up the Ghost

In 2004, the ghost of Indiana man Collin Proctor, in the form of his walking-cane, was sold on auction website eBay for $65,100 (£34,500). Mary Anderson of Hobart, Indiana, put her father's ghost up for sale to help her young son to cope with his grandfather's death. She asked the buyer to write to the boy acknowledging receipt of the ghost. Sadly, the sale came back to haunt her as the resultant publicity gave her insomnia.

Tunnel Vision

The driver of this car was caught in a sticky situation after mistaking the entrance to the subway for a ramp into a parking garage in Paris, France. Firemen were called in to rescue the car from slipping further down into the underground tunnels.

The Price You Pay

A St. Louis janitor got his finger stuck in a pay-phone change slot and spent three hours trying to dislodge it while passers-by laughed at his predicament. He finally thought to use his free hand to call 911.

Sweet Dreams

A Japanese toy firm claims to have devised a gadget that can help people to control their dreams. They say the Dream Workshop can be programmed before bedtime to help sleepers choose who or what they want to dream about.

Chin Up

Robert Dotzauer from Los Angeles could balance three lawnmowers on his chin at the same time.

Fending Off Sharks

THANKS TO THE Shark Shield, shark attacks could soon become a thing of the past.

The new invention, from Australian company SeaChange Technology, emits an electronic field to repel sharks without harming them. It can be fitted to surfboards or to divers' legs to allow people to enjoy the water without risk of attack.

The device emits an electronic field that will cause nearby sharks to have muscular spasms. This will put them off venturing closer, but doesn't cause any lasting damage.

Emergency Service
Policemen who arrested a burglar on the roof of a bank in Kent, England, had to be rescued by fire crews after they became stuck.

In the Hot Seat
Around the time of the invention of the electric chair, an unwitting citizen in New York State offered to test the electric current in the chair: the current worked and the man's family received $5,000 (£2,650).

I'm All Ears
The exhibition, entitled "Show and Tel: the Art of Connection," held at the Zimmer Children's Museum in Los Angeles, California, included quirky designs such as this two-part ear-and-mouthpiece telephone by Robert Graham.

Zimmer Frame
"Commander Ian Zimmer," designed by Alan and Deborah Ladwig, is just one of the bizarre telephonic inventions that were on display.

Does It Bite?
Should you stroke it or answer it? The phones, like this one by Mauro Caputo, were later auctioned.

Ring My Bell
Wedding bells won't be the only bells ringing on this telephone, created by Jessica Trovato. The designers of the unusual creations at the exhibition included athletes, politicians, and celebrities, such as Elizabeth Taylor, Alicia Keys, and Paula Abdul.

Water World

If you're the type of person who envies the life of a fish, then the hemosponge invention may be just for you! It's an experimental device created by the U.S. Office of Naval Research, that extracts oxygen from the water, making it possible for divers to remain submerged for several days at a time.

Fall Guy

Brazilian Marcello Bonga made the first ever crossing by rope of the Iguazu waterfalls from the Brazilian side to the Argentinian side. He crossed the Devil's Throat section, using only a rope and a harness, as thousands of tons of water crashed beneath him.

InDex

ACKNOWLEDGMENTS

10 (l, r) and 11 (t/l & r) Erik S. Lesser; 13 (b) Peter Macdiarmid/REUTERS; 14 (b) Brian Harris/Rex Features; 15 (l, t/r & b/r) Colin Shepherd/Rex Features; 16 (b/r) Lehtikuva Oy/Rex Features; 17 (t) Universal Orlando/Kevin Kolczynski/REUTERS; 18 (t/r) Huw Evans/Rex Features; 19 Stewart Cook/Rex Features; 20 (t/r) © Amy C. Elliot; 23 (t/l) Denis Closon/Rex Features, (b) Shaun Best/REUTERS; 26 (t) Sipa Press/Rex Features; 27 (t/r) Nick Young Bateman/Rex Features, (b/r) Features North/Rex Features; 28 (t/r) Peter Brooker/Rex Features, (b/l) Luis Enrique Ascui/REUTERS, (b/r) Phil Yeomans/Rex Features; 30 (t/l) Francois Lenoir/REUTERS, (b/l) Lefevre Sylvain/Sipa/Rex Features; 32 (l) Sipa Press/Rex Features; 33 (b) STR/REUTERS; 34 (b) Peter Brooker/Rex Features; 35 Brandi Easter, Arcata, Calif. U.S.A.; 36 (b/c) Chris Hellier/Rex Features; 37 (b/r) REUTERS; 38–39 Eric C Pendzich/Rex Features; 40 (c) Mike Carmichael; 42 (c/l) Ralph Merlino/Rex Features, (b) Nils Jorgensen/ Rex Features; 43 (t & b) Drew Gardner/ Rex Features; 44 (b) SWS/Rex Features; 45 (t/r) Tim Shaffer/REUTERS, (b) ZZ/XXD/SPL /Rex Features; 47 Lee Besford/REUTERS; 48 (t/r) JZB/Rex Features, (b/l) Dan Charity/ Rex Features; 49 (b) John Gurzinski /AFP/GETTYIMAGE; 50 (t/r) Nils Jorgensen/Rex Features; 51 (t/l) Mark Mawson/ Rex Features, (b) Shannon Stapleton/REUTERS; 52 (b) Getty Images; 53 (t/l) Alban Donohoe/Rex Features; 54 (b/l) Lindsey Parnaby/Rex Features; 55 (t/r) Action Press/Rex Features, (b/c) ACM/UTN/ZZ/Rex Features; 56 Boston Herald/Rex Features; 57 Eric C Pendzich/Rex Features; 58 (t/l) Simon Jones/Rex Features, (b) Stringer/India/REUTERS; 59 (t) Geoff Wilkinson/Rex Features; 61 (t/r) Brendan Beirne/Rex Features, (b) SWS/Rex Features; 62 (t/l) Jagadeesh NV/REUTERS; 63 (t/l) Peter Brooker/Rex Features, (b/r) Doug Hall/Rex Features; 64 (t/l) Sukree Sukplang/REUTERS, (b/r) Nils Jorgensen/Rex Features; 65 (c) MY/NAP/Rex Features; 67 Ali Jarekji/REUTERS; 70 (t/r & b/c) Tony Larkin/Rex Features; 71 (t/r) A Rodriguez/Rex Features, (b/r) EDPpics/Hocknell/Rex Features; 72 (b) Henry Romero/REUTERS; 73 (t) Adrian Sherratt/Rex Features; 75 (t/r) Mimmo Frassineti/Rex Features, (b/l) Paul Cooper/Rex Features; 76 (t/r) Assignments Photographers/Rex Features, (b/c) Toshifiumi Kitamura/AFP/GETTYIMAGE; 77 (b) 24/7 Media/Rex Features; 78 (b) Mike Walker/Rex Features; 79 (t/r & b) Nigel Tisdall/Rex Features; 80 (t/l) NWI/Rex Features; 81 SWS/Rex Features; 82 (b) Ian Patrick/Rex Features; 83 (t/r) Brendan Beirne/Rex Features; 86 (b) Assignments Photographers/Rex Features; 87 (b) John Chapple/Rex Features; 88 (t/r) HO/REUTERS, (b) Sipa Press/Rex Features; 89 (b) Eriko Sugita/REUTERS; 91 (t/r & b/r) Nils Jorgensen/Rex Features, (c) Gerry Penny/AFP/GETTYIMAGE Photo; 92 Ray Tang/Rex Features; 93 Rex Features; 94 (dps & b) Norm Betts/Rex Features; 96 (t/r & c) REUTERS, (b) Rowan Griffiths/Rex Features; 100-101 *Echo and Narcissus*, Utah Arts Festival, Salt Lake City, Utah, Photo and Design © Kurt Wenner, 100 *Saint Francis Preaches to the Fish*, Santa Barbara, California, Photo and Design © Kurt Wenner, 101 *Merchant of Venice*, Festa Italiana, Portland, Oregon, Photo and Design © Kurt Wenner: for more information: www.kurtwenner.com; 103 (b) Mark Campbell/Rex Features; 104 (t) Rob Howarth/Rex Features, (b) Fatih Saribas/REUTERS; 105 (t) PB/Rex Features, (b) Rex Features; 106 (full & b) Erik C Pendzich/Rex Features; 107 (b/r) Daniela Larini/Rex Features; 108 (b) Sam Tinson/Rex Features; 110 (t) Lindsay Hebberd/Corbis; 111 (b) Lewis Durham/Rex Features; 112 Joel W Rogers/Corbis; 113 (t) Toby Melville/REUTERS, (b/l) Stringer/REUTERS; 116 (b/l) Claro Cortes/REUTERS; 119 (l) REUTERS, (r) Peter Brooker/Rex Features; 120 (t) B Mathur/REUTERS; 121 Karl Schoendorfer/Rex Features; 122 (t/l) REUTERS, (b/l) Kamal Kishore/REUTERS; 123 (b) Tobias Schwarz/REUTERS; 124 (b/c) Savita Kirloskar/REUTERS, (b/r) Sherwin Crasto/REUTERS; 126 (b) Ponopresse/Rex Features; 127 (t) Richard Crampton/Rex Features, (b/r) Sipa Press/Rex Features; 130 (b) Paul Cooper/Rex Features; 131 (t/c) Rex Features, (c) Drew Gardner/Rex Features; 132 (t/l, t/c & t/r) Mike Walker/Rex Features; 133 (c) Leon Schadeberg/Rex Features, (b) Masatoshi Okauchi/Rex Features; 134 Issei Kato/REUTERS; 137 (t/l) Kimimasa Mayama/REUTERS, (b) Alex Grimm/REUTERS; 138 (b) REUTERS; 139 (t/r) Simon Kwong/REUTERS, (c) HO/REUTERS; 140 (b) Mark Campbell/Rex Features; 141 (t/r & c) Andy Newman/AFP/GETTYIMAGE; 142 John Chapple/Rex Features, (b/r) AFP/GETTYIMAGE; 143 (t/l) Paul Jones/AFP/GETTYIMAGE, (b) Simon Baker/REUTERS; 146 (b) Getty Images; 147 (t) Paul Cooper/Rex Features, (b) EDPPics/Usher/Rex Features; 148 (b) Rex Features; 149 (b) Phil Yeomans/Rex Features; 150 (b/c) Alisdair Macdonald/Rex Features; 151 (t/r) Tim Wimborne/REUTERS, (c) Dan Riedlhuber/REUTERS, (c/l) Rex Features; 152 (t/c & t/r) Courtesy of Sharon Robinson, (b/r) John O Reilley/Rex Features; 154 Rex Features; 155 Kevin Wisniewski/Rex Features; 156 (b) Paul Nicholls/Rex Features; 157 (t/l) Sukree Sukplang/REUTERS, (b) REUTERS; 160 Sam Barcroft/Rex Features; 162 (t/l & b/r) Marcos Brindicci/REUTERS; 163 (b) Action Press/Rex Features; 164 (t) Masatoshi Okauchi/Rex Features, (b) Alessia Pierdomenico/REUTERS; 166 (b) Desmond Boylan/REUTERS; 167 (t) STR/REUTERS, (b) Sipa Press/Rex Features; 169 Erika Nelson/World's Largest Things/www.WorldsLargestThings.com; 170 (t) David Loh/REUTERS; 171 (t/r) Chip East/REUTERS, (b) Romeo Ranoco/REUTERS; 172 (b/l) "Red Boots Productions", Hollywood, CA, USA, (r) "Wonders of Science", Whittier, CA, USA; 173 (t) Andrea/Rex Features. (b) Stringer/REUTERS; 176 (t) Matt Cardy/Rex Features; 177 (b) Adrian Sherratt/Rex Features; 178 (dps) Paul Gillis/Rex Features, (b) MMP/NAP/Rex Features; 179 (t) United Television News/Rex Features, (c) South West News/Rex Features, (b) HO/REUTERS; 180 (b) Dan Riedlhuber/REUTERS; 181 George A. Blair; 182 (full) SCANPIX /REUTERS; 183 (t) Howard Walker/Rex Features, (b) Picture Partnership/Rex Features; 184 (t/c & t/r) Phil Yeomans/Rex Features, (b) John Powell/Rex Features; 185 © Amy C. Elliot; 186 (b) Sipa Press/Rex Features; 187 (t) Andrew Winning/REUTERS, (b) Action Press/Rex Features; 193 (b) Ray Tang/Rex Features; 194 (t) Nils Jorgensen/Rex Features, (b) Northscot Press Agency/Rex Features; 195 (t) Charles M. Ommanney/Rex Features, (b) Greg Williams/Rex Features; 196 (t) David Bebber/REUTERS; 197 (t) David Grey/REUTERS; 198 (t) Action Press/Rex Features, (b) TDY/Rex Features; 200 (t) Stills Press Agency/Rex Features; 201 (b) Romeo Ranoco/REUTERS; 206 (b) Nils Jorgensen/Rex Features; 207 (t/r) Stringer/REUTERS, (b) Stringer/REUTERS; 208 (c & b) SWS/Rex Features; 209 (t/r) Kimberly White/REUTERS; 210 (t) Ken McKay/Rex Features, (b) Sipa Press/Rex Features; 211 (c/l) Peter Lomas/Rex Features; 212 (t) HO/REUTERS; 213 (b) Phil Yeomans/Rex Features; 214 (t) Jennifer Podis/Rex Features, (b) Rex Features; 215 Mike Blake/REUTERS; 216 (t) Patrick Barth/Rex Features, (b) Rex Features; 217 (b) David Hartley/Rex Features; 220 (dps) Lewis Whyld/Rex Features; 221 (t/l) Lewis Whyld/Rex Features, (t/r & b/r) Inflate/Rex Features; 222 (b) Sam Barcroft/Rex Features; 223 (t/l) Rex Features, (b/r) REUTERS; 224 (t/r) SON/NAP/Rex Features; 225 (full) Kim Kyung-Hoon/REUTERS, (b/l) Yuriko Nakao/REUTERS; 226 (t/r) United National Photographers/Rex Features; 227 (t/r & b) Anuruddha Lokuhapuarachchi/REUTERS; 229 Nils Jorgensen/Rex Features; 230 (t/r) Anuruddha Lokuhapuarachchi/REUTERS; 231 (full) Allover Norway/Rex Features, (t/r) Soren Nielsen/Rex Features, (b/r) Morten Nordby/Rex Features; 232 (b/l) Simon Kwong/REUTERS; 233 (t/r & b/l) David Gray/REUTERS; 236 (t/l) Darren Banks/Rex Features, (c/r) Mike Poloway/Rex Features, (b) United National Photographers/Rex Features; 240 (b/l) Sipa Press/Rex Features, (b/r) HOM/Rex Features; 242 (t) John Downing/Rex Features, (b/r) Sukree Sukplang/REUTERS; 243 South West News Service/Rex Features; 244 (t/l) Sipa Press/Rex Features; 245 Rex Features; 246 Peter Brooker/Rex Features; 247 Jon Super/Rex Features.

All other photos are from MKP Archives, PhotoDisc, and Ripley's Entertainment Inc.

Every attempt has been made to contact the copyright holders and we apologize in advance for any unintentional omissions.